WOMEN IN
SCIENCE

Jane Goodall
*Primatologist and
UN Messenger of Peace*

Cavendish
Square

New York

Megan Mitchell

Published in 2017 by Cavendish Square Publishing, LLC
243 5th Avenue, Suite 136, New York, NY 10016

Copyright © 2017 by Cavendish Square Publishing, LLC

First Edition

Library of Congress Cataloging-in-Publication Data

Names: Mitchell, Megan.
Title: Jane Goodall : primatologist and UN messenger of peace / Megan Mitchell.
Description: New York : Cavendish Square Publishing, [2017] | Series: Women in science | Includes bibliographical references and index.
Identifiers: LCCN 2016029412 (print) | LCCN 2016029940 (ebook) | ISBN 9781502623157 (library bound) | ISBN 9781502623164 (E-book)
Subjects: LCSH: Goodall, Jane, 1934---Juvenile literature | Primatologists--England--Biography--Juvenile literature. | Women primatologists--England--Biography--Juvenile literature.
Classification: LCC QL31.G58 M58 2017 (print) | LCC QL31.G58 (ebook) | DDC 599.8092 [B] --dc23
LC record available at https://lccn.loc.gov/2016029412

Editorial Director: David McNamara
Editors: Elizabeth Schmermund
Copy Editor: Rebecca Rohan
Associate Art Director: Amy Greenan
Designer: Alan Sliwinski
Production Assistant: Karol Szymczuk
Photo Research: J8 Media

The photographs in this book are used by permission and through the courtesy of: Cover, p. 73 CBS Photo Archive/Getty Images; Ian Waldie/Getty Images, background design used on cover and throughout; p. 4 Attila Kisbenedek/AFP/Getty Images; p. 8 Alberto E. Rodriguez/Getty Images; p. 15 National Aeronautics and Space Administration/[1] (http://www.lib.utexas.edu/maps/africa/kenya.gif) from the Perry-Castañeda Library Map Collection (http://www.lib.utexas.edu/maps/kenya.html)/File: Kenya Map.png/ Wikimedia Commons/Public Domain; p. 18 Hulton Archive/Archive Photos/Getty Images; p. 20 Science Source/Getty Images; pp. 22-23 General Photographic Agency/Hulton Archive/Getty Images; pp. 24-25 Fox Photos/Hulton Archive/Getty Images; p. 26 The National Archives/SSPL/Getty Images; pp. 30-31 Arthur Tanner/Fox Photos/Hulton Archive/Getty Images; p. 46 J. Erxleben/http:// www.lib.utexas.edu/books/britfossils/html/txu-oclc-13370987-2-dinosauria-plate29.php/File: Megalosaurus femur.jpg/Wikimedia Commons/Public Domain; pp. 54-55 Didier Descouens/Own work/File: Australopithecus africanus - Cast of taung child.jpg/ Wikimedia Commons/CCA-SA 4.0 International; p. 57 Daderot/File:Homo habilis skull - Naturmuseum Senckenberg - DSC02097. JPG/Wikimedia Commons/CC0 1.0 Universal Public Domain Dedication; p. 65 Cyril Ruoso/Minden Pictures/Getty Images; p. 67 DLILLC/Corbis/VCG/Getty Images; p. 68 Bettmann/Getty Images; p. 76 © CSU Archives/Everett Collection/Alamy Stock Photo; p. 82 Penelope Breese/Liaison/Hulton Archive/Getty Images; p. 88 Anup Shah/Getty Images; p. 94 Ronald Wittek/Getty Images; p. 97 Suzanne Plunkett/AFP/Getty Images; p. 99 Gustavo Caballero/Getty Images; p. 104 United News/Popperfoto/Getty Images.

Printed in the United States of America

CONTENTS

Jane Goodall has dedicated her life to the study of chimpanzees. A champion of animal rights and environmental protection, her work has impacted the fields of paleoanthropology, zoology, and genetics.

INTRODUCTION

JANE GOODALL AT THE PEAK

Crouched in the grass, the young woman cautiously crept forward, not wishing to scare the two chimpanzees sitting a few yards away. One of the chimps had a scruffy patch of gray hair on his chin, earning him the nickname "David Greybeard." Through binoculars, she patiently observed the two primates, ignoring the buzzing of insects surrounding her and the humid heat of the mountainous jungle. Before leaving on her expedition to study chimpanzees in the wild, the young woman, Jane Goodall, a thoughtful, adventurous scientist from Britain, had received instructions from her mentor to not only carefully watch and record all behaviors that she observed, but also to look for signs of tool use among the chimpanzees. At the time, it was widely believed that humans were the only animals crafty enough to use objects consciously, but Louis Leakey, Goodall's mentor, felt differently.

Goodall had already been in the field now for three months. Each morning, she rose at 5:30 a.m., quickly eating a breakfast of bread and coffee before climbing the slopes surrounding her research camp. As she made her ascent each morning, she watched the sun rise and the jungle wake up around her. The treks were challenging; her route was steep, and the heat of the jungle permeated soon after sunrise. She spent most of her days crawling through the brush, her clothes and body covered in dirt, leaves and vines tangled in her hair. In spite of it all, the young woman loved each moment of her fieldwork. Early on, she discovered a spot where the tribe of chimpanzees visited almost daily. Nicknamed the Peak, Goodall observed the chimps there almost each day. She even began naming them, often after people that she knew. Mr. McGregor, William, Olly and her daughter Flo, David Greybeard, and Goliath became fixtures in Goodall's observation notebooks. Each had his or her own personality; William, for instance, was aggressive and even though Goodall only acted as a silent observer, would often shake tree branches near her in an attempt to scare her off. It didn't work, though. She continued her routine, hoping to see the chimps engaging in never-before-recorded behaviors. Several such observations would occur in the young scientist's career, one of the first being with the chimps David Greybeard and Goliath, named for his large size.

On that particular day, Goodall sat watching the two; David was perched atop a large termite mound. Through her binoculars, Jane could see the chimps pushing blades of grass in the opening at the top of the hill and then removing them. Eventually, the two wandered off and, curious, Goodall went to investigate. She realized that the two had been using the grass to extract termites, a tasty snack for chimpanzees. David and Goliath were using tools! Excitedly, she rushed back to camp to telegraph her mentor the surprising news, for this would be the first time wild chimpanzees were observed using tools. Through this discovery and many other contributions, Jane Goodall would become one of the most well-known and beloved scientists, activists, and spokespersons for animal rights and environmental conservation. The following chapters will explore her childhood and her early years in the field. We'll examine the history of studying primates and what was going on in the world as young Goodall began her research. Finally, we'll explore her impact today through her many awards, recognitions, and publications.

The gift of a stuffed chimpanzee helped pique Jane's interest in studying wildlife as a young girl.

A NATURALIST IS BORN

Mortimer Morris-Goodall and Margaret Myfanwe Joseph, nicknamed Vanne, welcomed their daughter Valerie Jane Morris-Goodall into the world at 11:30 p.m. on Tuesday, April 3, 1934, in a London hospital. Little Valerie Jane entered a world of motor oil and excitement. Her father, Mortimer, had a passion for Aston Martin race cars and, in 1933, joined the car company's racing team. Married in 1932, Vanne did not share her adventurous husband's passion for fast cars but supported his new career. Mortimer would eventually be recognized as a skilled driver and participate in the tough Le Mans Grand Prix race ten times.

Goodall developed a love for animals early in life. On her first birthday, Mortimer purchased a unique toy for his tiny daughter. That year, 1935, England joyfully welcomed Jubilee, the first baby chimpanzee born in captivity at the London Zoo. Goodall's father bought her a lifelike, stuffed chimp; named after the new zoo baby, the toy quickly became the little girl's favorite.

Her fascination did not end with her new stuffed friend. Vanne encouraged her young daughter to explore the family's back garden and local parks. Goodall delighted in hunting for earthworms and playing with the family dog, a bull terrier named Peggy.

The arrival of younger sister Judith Daphne, born on Valerie Jane's fourth birthday in 1938, disrupted her happy world. As an older sister, she was at first skeptical of the infant but soon accepted Judith as part of her small family. As the two grew older, their father's racing career continued to grow, and when Valerie Jane was five, Mortimer moved the family to France to focus on his career. However, the move was short-lived. As Europe descended into war, safety became a major concern for the family, and they moved back to England.

Despite the uncertainties of being a young girl in the midst of a world at war, Goodall continued to learn about the natural world. Back in England, the Morris-Goodall family moved in with Vanne's mother, affectionately called "Danny Nutt" because young Valerie Jane could not pronounce Granny. She would later recall:

> ❝ The manor house was way out in the country, with a big farm next door. On the grounds were the ruins of a castle where the wicked king, Henry VIII, had shut up one of his wives. I remember those ruins: they seemed scary, all gray, crumbling stone and spider webs … The manor house itself was very old, too. If you walked from one end to the other, you had to go down one or two steps here, up a little there, and so on, because different parts had been built at different times. It was made of gray stone, which was cool

in summer and very cold in winter. There was no central heating. There were few places in England with central heating in those days. **"**

The time spent at her grandmother's house was one of exploration. Later, Goodall would recall about living with her mother and grandmother:

" *How would I have turned out, I sometimes wonder, had I grown up in a house that stifled enterprise by imposing harsh and senseless discipline? Or in an atmosphere of overindulgence, in a household where there were no rules, no boundaries drawn? My mother certainly understood the importance of discipline, but she always explained why some things were not allowed. Above all, she tried to be fair and to be consistent.* **"**

Danny Nutt assigned her granddaughter the chore of collecting the eggs from the henhouse. How on earth, the young girl wondered, did such small birds produce such large eggs? Goodall decided to wait quietly in the henhouse to try and witness the strange event. Finally, after four hours, a hen settled into a nest and laid a perfect egg. The young scientist raced home to excitedly tell Vanne. She would later recall:

" *That is the exact makings of a little scientist, curiosity, asking questions, watching. If you don't get the answer to the question, find out a way of doing it, so you are finding out for yourself. If that doesn't work, try again.* **"**

Goodall also kept a **menagerie** of various insects and other curious animals. Her collection included snails, guinea pigs, moths, and a legless lizard named Ivor Novello.

The family also had dogs, and Valerie Jane rode horses. In addition to her caretaking responsibilities, the young girl was an avid reader. Her favorite stories involved animals; the world of Dr. Doolittle, a veterinarian who could speak to animals, Tarzan's exotic jungle, and Rudyard Kipling's *Jungle Book* were among her childhood favorites.

At the age of twelve, Goodall founded the Alligator Club. The nature group met regularly to walk and play outdoors and organize fundraisers for elderly horses; they also produced *The Alligator Letter*, a series of drawings and articles written by the club members, each with her own nature nickname. As the leader, Goodall selected the Red Admiral, a species of butterfly, to be her moniker.

TROUBLE AT HOME

Even though Valerie Jane flourished in the outdoors, all was not well in the Morris-Goodall household. Although he demonstrated expertise on the racetrack, Mortimer struggled with money management, causing problems at home. Around Goodall's fifth birthday, her father enlisted in the military as a British officer. He was soon deployed to France to fight the advancing German forces. His military service continued with assignments to China and India. The trips home became fewer and fewer and, near the end of the war, Vanne and Mortimer divorced.

EDUCATION

Goodall began school at the age of six in 1940. In addition to reading nature stories, the young student also enjoyed writing stories about animals. "The Silly Giraffe," her first story, was written in 1941 when she was seven years old. She would continue to write poetry and stories throughout her formal education.

In 1945, she attended the all-girls' Uplands School. There she took advanced science courses, although she wasn't particularly fond of the coursework, writing in her diary that physics could be "crazy" and chemistry felt "pointless" at times. It was during this time that Valerie Jane felt a shift in her identity and began referring to herself as just Jane. In 1951, she graduated and was invited to live with family members in Germany for four months. Upon her return, Vanne suggested that her daughter enroll in secretarial school. The Queen's Secretarial College trained women in typing and shorthand, and in 1954, Goodall completed her courses and moved to Oxford to work in the Oxford University Registry. She worked there for a short time and then moved to London to work at a documentary film company.

Goodall loved living independently. She took up residence in a tiny basement apartment and spent her time off work making new friends and exploring the city. She still felt restless and unsatisfied. Despite her new adult life, something was missing. A year earlier, her friend from Uplands, Marie-Claude Mange, had written to invite Goodall to her family's farm in Nairobi, Kenya. Now, the offer seemed more tempting than ever.

On March 13, 1957, Goodall boarded the *Kenya Castle*, a 17,000-ton passenger steamship bound for Kenya. Around one month later, on April 2, the enormous boat docked at Mobasa, Kenya. Goodall then boarded a train for Nairobi and would arrive in her new home in the early hours of April 3, her 22nd birthday.

Kenya

Characterized as the "cradle of humanity," Kenya is an East African country bordered by Somalia, Ethiopia, Uganda, and Tanzania, with a coastline on the Indian Ocean. The country's landscapes include savannahs, lakelands, mountainous terrain, and the Great Rift Valley. The Great Rift Valley is a 3,700-mile (5,955-kilometer) trench that extends from Asia to Mozambique in southern East Africa. Kenya is also home to wildlife such as elephants, chimpanzees, lions, and rhinos.

It was into this new world, so different than rainy London, that Goodall arrived at her friend's family farm outside of Nairobi, the country's capital. However excited she was to observe wildlife and explore the countryside, Kenya's political climate at the time was tumultuous. Under British rule, Kenya's desire for independence violently culminated with the assassination of a prominent British supporter by rebels in 1952. The British government declared Kenya to be in a state of emergency, a chaotic pronouncement that would last for nearly eight years. British troops were sent, and many Kenyans were arrested. Mau Mau rebels continued to act violently, but most often against the native Kikuyu tribe who had long cooperated with the British, despite there being Kikuyu members on the rebel side as well. Eventually, the imperialist nation relinquished control of the

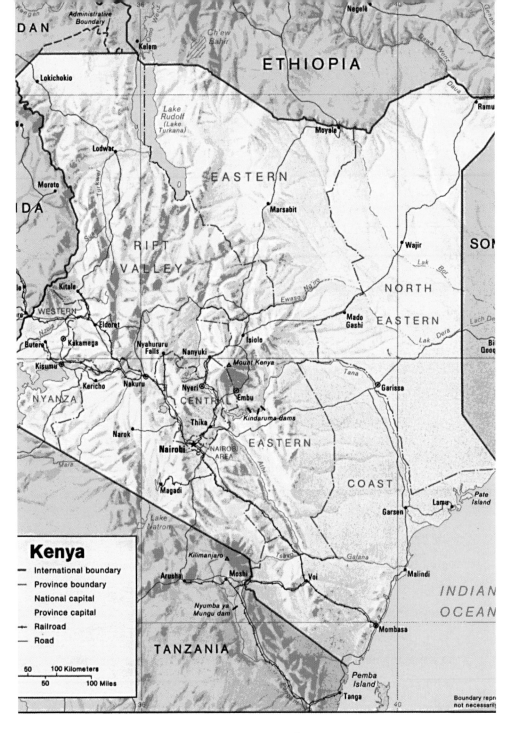

Kenya, the first African country that Jane visited, covers over 200,000 square miles (517,998 square kilometers) and is home to over 44 million people.

African country, and Kenya declared itself an independent country on December 12, 1963.

Although the violence and bloodshed of these years served as a backdrop to Goodall's time in Kenya, she enjoyed exploring the Manges' farm, and her desire to work with animals grew. Goodall wanted to stay in Kenya and began looking for a job. She found a position as a secretary for a British firm in Nairobi. While it allowed her to live independently, Goodall still longed to work with the local wildlife. She began to hear from several acquaintances that, if she wanted to work with animals, she needed to speak to a man named Dr. Louis Leakey.

LOUIS LEAKEY

A prominent scientist in Kenya, Louis Leakey had quite an impressive resume. He had earned a PhD from Cambridge University and an honorary Doctor of Science degree from Oxford University. Based on his work in **paleoanthropology**, the study of the evolution of humans, Dr. Leakey was highly regarded both in Kenya and the larger scientific community. One of Goodall's friends, who worked with Leakey at Nairobi's first natural history museum, promised to mention her name to the scientist, but Goodall grew impatient and called the museum herself. Although she received an initial grumpy response, with the great scientist returning her call and saying "What do you want?," Leakey invited the young woman to the museum and the two hit it off during a tour and conversation. He hired Goodall as his secretary, and they soon developed a strong teacher-student relationship. Goodall even accompanied Leakey's team to a paleo-dig for three months. During this time, Leakey advocated his belief in the need for in-depth primate studies. Leakey believed that apes, like chimpanzees and gorillas, were vital to understanding early human behaviors.

When Goodall boldly asked her mentor to allow her to conduct research on chimpanzees, he gleefully replied: "Why on earth did you think I talked about those chimpanzees to you?" Although the young scientist worried about her lack of education credentials, Leakey believed she was the perfect candidate and would enter the field unaltered by particular scientific theories or other researchers' work.

Securing funding would take a long time, so Leakey sent Goodall back to London to begin studying chimpanzees. Despite criticism and shock from the scientific community, Leakey secured permission for Goodall to study at the Gombe Stream Game Reserve, but the British official who gave the approval demanded that she have a chaperone. The perfect choice, it turned out, was Vanne, Goodall's loving mother.

GOMBE

The funding secured by Leakey came from Leighton Wilkie, an Illinois businessman interested in human evolution. Because the British government in Kenya refused to allow Goodall to travel on the expedition alone, her mother volunteered to accompany her. In July 1960, Vanne and Jane left London and journeyed 800 miles (1,287 km) over dirt roads to Lake Tanganyika. Political unrest in the area meant the duo waited two weeks before embarking on a small, aluminum boat twelve miles (19 km) to the Gombe Stream Game Reserve.

Located on the east side of the lake, the Reserve measured about ten miles (16 km) from north to south. The surrounding environment, a lakeshore on one side and cultivated farmland creating the boundary

LOUIS LEAKEY

Harry and May Leakey welcomed their son, Louis, on April 7, 1903, as missionaries living in Kenya. Little Louis had two older sisters and soon after his younger brother was born, Mrs. Leakey hired a local nanny, Mariamu. Louis spent his childhood hearing animal folktales from Mariamu and caring for orphaned baby animals like monkeys and gazelles. Simultaneously, he learned Latin, mathematics, and French from tutors.

At the age of sixteen, Leakey attended school in London after his family returned for several years and matriculated to Cambridge to study paleoanthropology. While at university, he formally studied Kikuyu, the native language spoken to him by Mariamu. At the age of twenty-one, Leakey returned to his beloved East Africa to head an archaeological dig. He was determined to study human evolution and would go on to revolutionize the field.

Louis Leakey's legacy continues today; his granddaughter, Louise Leakey, researches human fossils found in Eastern Africa.

on the other, created an isolated ecosystem home estimated to be home to about 160 chimps. Other primates, like baboons, inhabited the region too.

Research

For the next three months, Goodall struggled to find chimpanzee groups and, once located, not scare them away. She did observe that the primates traveled in different-sized groups but began to worry that she would not be able to get close enough to observe any significant behaviors. A breakthrough, though, was soon to come.

Marie Curie conducted the majority of her research in France but never forgot her Polish roots. In fact, she named the first chemical element she discovered, polonium, after her home country, which she left at age twenty-four.

CHAPTER TWO

JANE GOODALL'S TIMES

Long before Jane made her first journey to Gombe, women were breaking barriers in math and science. From the late 1600s to the early 1800s, women held professorships at universities in Europe and contributed to many discoveries. Caroline Herschel, for instance, was appointed as chief assistant to her brother William Herschel, a prominent astronomer, in the late 1700s. Caroline discovered several comets, wrote and published articles, and performed the calculations for her brother's studies. However, the path to scientific freedom and recognition was long. Elizabeth Blackwell, the first woman to officially obtain a medical degree, became a doctor in 1849; she was preceded by James Barry, born Margaret Ann Buckley, who lived as a man in order to attend medical school when women were prohibited.

Marie Curie is recognized as a trailblazer for women in science. In 1903, she and her husband Pierre were jointly awarded the Nobel Prize in Physics and, in 1911, Marie became the first person to be awarded two Nobel prizes. Her second, in Chemistry, was awarded for the discovery of the radioactive elements radium and plutonium.

In addition to rejecting the more conservative fashion of earlier decades, flappers advocated for women's rights and working outside the home, a drastic change from the more divided gender roles of the older Victorian generation.

However, despite the successes of early female pioneers, access to the professional world was limited for women. Often, recognition and accolades were attributed to male scientists, even if their female colleagues aided their research.

THE 1920S AND 1930S

The Roaring Twenties replaced the restrictions and privacy of the Victorian era. In a time of economic prosperity, women acquired the right to vote in many countries. Flappers, women who went against traditional gender roles, danced to jazz music, cut their hair short, and wore short dresses. Female college attendance increased, and the invention of the automobile created more freedom for young people.

The excess of the 1920s, however, quickly came to a halt in 1929. The Great Depression, the worst economic downturn in recent history, lasted for a decade and included extremely high unemployment rates, reduced spending, and increased poverty. Roles of men and women quickly became divided; for women who worked, many viewed their employment as competition for men when jobs were scarce. A famous American journalist commented, "Simply fire the women, who shouldn't be working anyway, and hire the men. Presto! No unemployment. No relief rolls. No depression." While employment rose for women during this time, it was mainly in secretarial and sales jobs, which reinforced divisions between women and men's labor.

THE WORLD AT WAR

While Goodall's childhood was full of exploration, the world around her was in crisis. On September 3, 1939, Britain and France declared war on Germany. The declaration followed the September 1 Nazi invasion of Poland. Citizens quickly began making thick, dark curtains to cover their windows in case of a bombing. The London Zoo closed, and sandbags were placed around buildings to protect them from potential attacks.

One of the first major causes of this declaration was the British passenger ship *Athenia*. A German submarine crew, believing the ship to be armed, sank the ocean liner, and 112 of the 1,100 passengers aboard died.

Six months later, in May 1940, the German army defeated the Allied forces and conquered France, Belgium, Luxembourg, and the Netherlands. The German occupation of France would last four years.

The "Blitz" damaged prominent areas of London; here, Big Ben and the Houses of Parliament serve as the backdrop to bombed, damaged buildings.

The evacuation of children from major English urban centers influenced many authors and was featured in works including C. S. Lewis's fantasy novel The Lion, the Witch, and the Wardrobe *and the children's book* Paddington Bear *by Michael Bond.*

While the Goodall family left France in 1939 to escape the escalating war, their home country of Britain was soon a prime target for the German military.

The Blitzkrieg

As a result of Great Britain's declaration of war on Germany, the German air force, called the Luftwaffe, began to attack British military bases. Adolf Hitler and other German military leaders planned to invade the island country, but when British forces resisted, the Luftwaffe changed tactics.

When German bomber planes appeared in the London skies on September 30, 1940, they initiated an attack on the capital city that would last for fifty-seven days. This tactical shift was intended to break the morale of the English and pressure the government to surrender to Germany.

For the next several weeks, the Luftwaffe attacked London night and day, starting fires and destroying buildings. Citizens took cover in underground subway stations and other buildings like schools. This was called the Blitzkrieg, meaning "lightning war" in German, and it was designed to cause chaos and fear.

Many Londoners, especially children, had evacuated before the Blitzkrieg. As early as September 1939, the British government encouraged parents to send their children away to the country for fear of civilian fatalities. But there were several waves of evacuation as well; overall, 3.5 million people would leave major British urban centers during this time.

WOMEN IN WARTIME

Britain called upon women in World War I to take on roles left behind by enlisted men and, as Germany's power grew in the Second World War, the country would once again depend on women's labor. In the spring of 1941, women between the ages of eighteen and sixty registered and interviewed for a range of wartime jobs. Officials emphasized that women should not be placed in conflict roles, but this was to change over the course of the war. When Britain declared war on Germany on September 3, 1939, Parliament passed the National Service Act (NSA), which required all men ages eighteen to sixty to register for **conscription.** A second NSA followed in 1941, making all childless or widowed women between the ages of twenty and thirty eligible for recruitment. While the act began with a limited scope, by 1943, a significant segment of the British female population was employed in war-related work.

Women's Land Army

As more British men left for military service, the need for labor in many industries soared. Agricultural jobs, in particular, were essential to Britain's economy, and food production was vital to the war effort. During World War I, Parliament established the Women's Land Army (WLA), which recruited women to fulfill many of the farming jobs left by drafted and enlisted male farm workers. In June 1939, the WLA was re-established. As part of the second National Service Act, women could choose between armed forces work or agricultural jobs. The 80,000 women working in the WLA by 1943 were nicknamed "Land Girls."

Land Girls came from all over the country; many left cities like London to go and live in the country for the first time. They lived on the farms where they worked or in special lodging called hostels. Land Girls performed many duties including harvesting, driving tractors, **animal husbandry**, farm maintenance, and timber production. They received little to no training and, often, their farm hosts were skeptical about the young, seemingly inexperienced workers. Pay was minimal, and the Land Girls worked through all seasons. Although the Women's Land Army sounds like a military branch, it was a civilian service. While the government centralized interviews, farmers directly recruited the women and were responsible for paying their workers. They could even dismiss Land Girls if they felt it was necessary to do so.

Despite farmers' initial doubts, as Germany and other **Axis countries** intensified their campaigns, the need for food production became more and more necessary. German U-boats, or military submarines, intercepted many supply ships from the United States and other **Allies** in the Atlantic Ocean, and Britain became more dependent on internal food production. By 1943, Land Girls produced enough food to sustain British troops. The Women's Land Army would continue feeding Britain after the war ended, until 1950, when it was disbanded.

WVS, WAAF, and Nurses

In addition to the Women's Land Army, there were many other roles fulfilled by women during World War II. The Women's Voluntary Services (WVS), founded in 1938, assisted in civilian evacuations, collecting clothes for the needy, and assisting with returning soldiers. They also provided support during the Blitzkrieg by distributing food and other supplies to civilians taking shelter from bomb raids.

Commanded by Katherine Trefusis-Forbes, the Women's Auxiliary Air Force (WAAF) began in 1939 with three primary goals: assisting with clerical work and delivering messages, driving, and cooking. WAAF roles expanded quickly. Women decrypted ciphers, or coded military messages, worked as engineers and mechanics

Nurses could be captured and held as prisoners of war (POW) alongside soldiers. One British nurse, Colonel Ruby Bradley, spent three years as a POW during World War II, caring for others in the camp.

on airplanes, and some even trained as agents to go undercover into Axis-occupied Europe. Although women of the WAAF did not fly airplanes, women in other organizations like the Air Transport Auxiliary did take on the role of pilot for non-combat purposes like shuttling planes back and forth for repair.

Female nurses also played a major role during World War II. They cared for wounded soldiers both in Britain and abroad, often in dangerous war zones. In 1941, a formal rank structure was initiated in which nurses could move through ranks that resembled those in the British Army.

Bomb Girls

In her book titled *Bomb Girls: Britain's Secret Army,* Jacky Hyams describes a secret, hidden army feverishly supporting Britain during the war. She writes:

“ *So who were they? They weren't code breakers, nor were they espionage agents working undercover. They didn't form part of some elite group operating behind* *the scenes. Yet effectively, theirs was a very significant hidden army, mostly female, teenage girls, young war brides, ordinary mums, war widows and even, in some instances, grandmothers. As Winston Churchill described them in a radio broadcast of 1940, their role was defined as 'soldiers with different weapons—but the same courage.' Unquestionably, without the work of this hidden female army, the story of the Second World War might have ended in a very different way.* **"**

Around 950,000 British women worked in munitions factories making artillery and weapons for the armed forces. The job was extremely dangerous, as the women worked around huge machinery and explosive material. Few of them received recognition for their work during or after the war.

WOMEN IN SCIENCE DURING WORLD WAR II

Across the Atlantic Ocean, women similarly filled roles left by American men drafted into the US armed forces. Additionally, women contributed to the Manhattan Project, the secret mission to design nuclear weapons.

Leona Woods was a physicist who was critical in discovering that nuclear weapons were feasible. Other female scientists contributed theoretical tests to the Manhattan Project. Maria Goeppert Mayer, who would later win a Nobel Prize in Physics, worked on nuclear explosion tests at Los Alamos National Laboratory for the United States war effort. Mathematicians, like Naomi Livesay, performed calculations at Los Alamos to track the shock waves of the experimental weapons. Lilli Hornig, a chemist, and a group of scientists tested explosions at the laboratory and were the assembly crew for the world's first nuclear explosion, organized under the code name Trinity in New Mexico in 1946.

Women were also critical in other wartime scientific advancements. Grace Murray Hopper worked as one of the first computer programmers for the US Navy. Hopper worked on Mark I, a large, automated calculator that predated modern computers. She coined the term "bug" to refer to computation machine problems after a moth disrupted Mark I's functioning.

GOODALL AND THE BIRCHES

Shortly after France and England signed a treaty to protect Poland against German invasion in May 1939, Mortimer and the other members of the Morris-Goodall family crossed the English Channel to settle in France so Mortimer could focus on his racing career.

Vanne experienced World War I as a child. Her brother, Eric, was shot down behind enemy lines in France but escaped with only a shattered ankle. Having lived through an event that killed many young British soldiers and was so traumatic that it was nicknamed "The Great War," Vanne felt it impossible that the world could go to war on such a scale again. However, out and about, the family began to notice the tension in the air; French and English soldiers were visible in many towns, and busy shops and beaches became less and less crowded. When Vanne received a telephone call from a family member with connections in the government, who urged the Morris-Goodalls to leave France, she immediately booked passage aboard a ship for Valerie Jane, Judith, and their nanny. She and Mortimer returned to England a few days later.

Soon after returning, Mortimer joined the British Army as an officer and left for France again. Vanne took the two girls to live with her mother in Bournemouth. The house, affectionately called The Birches, was situated among cliffs and beaches. Signs of the war still surrounded the family; because the area provided potential access for invading forces, large machine guns stood guard over the cliffs and minefields were laid. Even at home, the family took precautions, with each family member assigned a gas mask and a small suitcase packed with provisions.

Soon after the German army invaded Norway, Denmark, Holland, and Belgium, they began their invasion of France. The Allied troops began to evacuate. In Bournemouth, exhausted soldiers began to arrive, but Mortimer was not among them. He eventually escaped France and visited the family once back in England, but he soon left for duties at the War Office. Mortimer would go on to be shipped to India as a major and eventually to Hong Kong as a lieutenant colonel in 1950.

But not all of the family would survive the war. Valerie Jane's Uncle Rex, a flight instructor for the Royal Air Force, was killed in 1942 when a student he was teaching froze, causing the airplane to crash.

Despite all the chaos going on in the world during that time, Goodall adored her grandmother's house. Danny Nutt was a strong-willed and religious woman with a big heart. Vanne's two sisters, Aunt Olly and Aunt Audrey, also lived with the family in the **matriarchal** home.

Judith and Valerie Ann had a playroom and enjoyed simple laughter and fun. The family did not have much money and were further restricted in what they could buy by rationing. England's Ministry of Food limited the amount of ham, sugar, and butter that families could buy.

As the Blitz began in London, other towns that held airfields or military bases were also bombed. Despite Bournemouth's location as a port town and the location of forces there, the Luftwaffe only dropped bombs on the area occasionally. Like many houses during this time, The Birches had its own bomb shelter. Equipped with blankets and canned food, it was very small, but the family would squeeze in together.

Although the house was never damaged during bombings, several instances frightened the family. Vanne would later recall that in one particular instance, Valerie Jane proclaimed that she did not mind bombs and was not going to go into the shelter. Soon after, bombs started to hit the cliffs surrounding the home, shaking the house and windows, teaching the young girl a profound lesson. Later, in her memoir *Reason for Hope*, Jane recalled,

> **❝** *[More] and more often we would hear the drone of a German plane and the thunder of an exploding bomb. We were fortunate, as nothing fell close enough to do damage. But the windows rattled loudly, and some panes of glass were cracked. How well I still remember the wailing of the air-raid warnings. They usually sounded sometime in the night for that was when the bombers came over. Then we had to leave our beds and huddle together in the little air-raid shelter that was erected in our house in the small room (once a maid's bedroom) that, even today, is known as the 'air-raid.' It was a low, steel-roofed cage about six feet by five feet and only four feet high. Thousands of these were issued to households who were living in potential danger zones. And there we had to stay—sometimes as many as six adults as well as we two children—until the welcome sound of the 'All Clear.'* **❞**

In another memory shared by Judith, the younger sister recalled spotting a plane from the garden. At the time, Judith was very young and thought the plane was dropping "papers," which were, in fact, bombs. The family was astonished when, one sunny afternoon, a smoking German bomber flew at a low level over the house, so close that they could see the pilot's face, before crashing into the ocean.

After the bombing of Pearl Harbor on December 7, 1941, American soldiers began to arrive in Bournemouth. A young American soldier, the son of a friend of Danny Nutt's deceased husband, visited the family while he was stationed in the town. Upon his departure, Valerie Jane promised to write, and it was her letter that would eventually be returned to the young soldier's mother upon the news of his death in battle.

Valerie Jane also played an important role for Judith, who began having nightmares about Adolf Hitler and the Germans as a result of the stresses of the war. When the four-year-old would wake up in the night crying, Valerie Jane would run in to comfort her and draw her pictures to place under her pillow.

The war taught the young girl lessons about thriftiness and simplicity. It also left her with hard lessons on the scope of human suffering and cruelty.

CHANGING EXPECTATIONS: 1950S AND BEYOND

As the world moved toward healing and recovery after World War II ended, women moved back into their domestic roles. Returning veterans resumed the agricultural and labor jobs that women had worked during the war.

The number of women who held jobs outside the home dropped significantly by 1950; this was especially true for married women with children. Some were fired, particularly in heavy industry, to make room for the returning veterans. Despite the undeniable contribution that women had made during the war, they were still regarded as inferior. In 1928, Parliament had passed the Equal Franchise Act, giving women the same voting rights as men, but there were still limited expectations for women. Few women enrolled in college, despite the Education Act passed in 1944, and, for many, marriage and a domestic life seemed the only option.

In a period of great economic post-war boom, there was a strong effort across the Allied nations to become "normal" once again. Families followed rigid structures; after getting married, men often worked outside of the home and were in charge of all legal documents and bank accounts. Women, on the other hand, often stayed at home to look after the children and perform household chores.

For women who did remain in the workforce, they most often took jobs that were labeled as "women's work" and worked as secretaries, midwives, cleaners, and nurses. As these jobs were viewed as less important and, often, income earned by women was seen as supplemental, women received much lower wages than men. It was assumed that a man's wages were enough to support a family and that women worked to pay for nonessential things like vacations.

Furthermore, some employers would fire women when they got married or became pregnant. Married women, in most cases, were not allowed to work as teachers or in clerical jobs. Although the Equal Pay Act, which required equitable pay regardless of gender, and the Sex Discrimination Act, which prohibited preferential treatment based on one's gender, were not passed until 1970 and 1975 respectively, there were a few early laws in Britain that helped women. Winston Churchill, the **Prime Minister** of Great Britain from

1941 to 1945 and 1951 to 1955, granted equal pay for all civil service, or central government, employees.

Jane Goodall, a Woman of Science

In addition to the flood of veterans returning to the workplace after the war, newly returned soldiers flocked back to universities, and particularly into science and mathematics courses. Women in scientific fields were often hired as research assistants, taught at women's colleges where there was less money for research, or did not receive the same prestige or pay as their male scientist colleagues. Many female scientists rejected the idea of scientific work combined with any kind of secretarial duties. Ruth O'Brien, a chemist for the United States Department of Agriculture, stated:

> *For a really able woman chemist bent on maintaining her professional dignity, it is definitely [offensive] to permit her to have anything to do with a typing job … [there is] an octopus-like tendency of the typewriter to wrap its arms around her and refuse to let her rise above it.*

Other female scientists also vocalized criticism of gender discrimination. In a speech to the American Association for the Advancement of Science in 1958, the chemist Betty Lou Raskin proclaimed,

> *They have made the mink coat, not the lab coat, our symbol of success. They've praised beauty, not brains. They've emphasized leisure time, not hard work and originality. As a result, today's schoolgirl thinks it far more exciting to serve tea on an airplane than to form a new lightweight plastic in the laboratory.*

As a young girl dreaming of studying animals during this time, Goodall also felt the burden of these gendered expectations. When she shared her dreams of Africa and studying biology with a career counselor, photography was suggested as an appropriate alternative. Pet portraits, the counselor reasoned, would allow Goodall the access to wildlife she desired. Rejecting that notion, Jane would enroll at a secretarial school at Vanne's suggestion. Her mother always told her daughter, "[If] you really want something, you work hard, you take advantage of the opportunity and you never give up. You will find a way."

Despite Goodall's initial experiences in jobs considered appropriate for women, as a secretary, waitress, and typist, and, eventually, as Louis Leakey's assistant, she held on to her dream of studying animals in the African wild.

Even when Goodall finally told Leakey about her dreams and he secured funding for her to travel to the Gombe Stream Game Reserve to study the chimpanzees there, there were still more obstacles for the young, female scientist. Geoffrey Browning, the British district commissioner in Tanganyika, whose approval was necessary to travel to Gombe, did not allow any European women to travel alone in the Tanganyikan jungles.

Leakey did not share many of his male colleagues' views of female scientists. In fact, he believed that women might be more successful in observing animals, and particularly primates, as he believed they would be less likely to provoke a male chimp's aggression. When Jane's mentor mentioned to Vanne that she'd need a chaperone to study in Gombe, her mother eagerly volunteered. In addition to navigating the scientific world and the Kenyan jungles as a woman, both Goodall's early travels to and her later studies at Gombe would be shaped by the surrounding political tensions of the two countries.

KENYAN INDEPENDENCE

When Goodall arrived in Kenya in 1957, she entered a newly independent country following years of conflict between the Mau Mau rebels, the British Empire, and the Kiyuyu tribe. The region had long been at the intersection of multiple cultures. The official language, **Swahili,** resulted from a mixture of Bantu, a language spoken by many tribes in eastern and south Africa, and Arabic. The Portuguese arrived in 1498, and the country came under Islamic control in the 1600s.

The British arrived in the late 1800s after European powers divided up eastern parts of the continent. With the establishment of the East African Protectorate in 1895, the British Parliament soon opened up the fertile highlands to British settlers. Although the area would not be declared an official colony until 1920, British settlers were allowed participation in the government, while the African and Asian inhabitants were excluded.

Land was the primary interest for the white settlers, and the British seized large portions from tribes such as the Kikyuyu. Many Kenyans were also forced or coerced into hard labor. Kikyuyus and other tribes formed the collective group, the Mau Mau, to resist British occupation. Britain declared an official emergency in October 1952 and sent British troops. In October 1953, a prominent Mau Mau leader, Jomo Kenyatta, was imprisoned for his association with the rebellion. Many Kikyuyu tribe members were moved to camps and screened for possible association with the Mau Maus. There were casualties on both sides; British civilians and military personnel were killed and Maus Maus and Kikyuyu tribal members were killed in battle or by capital punishment. The conflict lasted until December 1959. Kenya went on to gain independence as a country in 1963, with Jomo Kenyatta as its first President.

TANZANIA

The Gombe Stream Game Reserve is located within Tanzania, a country that borders Kenya at its northern boundary and the Indian Ocean on the east. When Goodall and her mother arrived in 1960, Tanzania did not yet exist. Instead, it was referred to as Tanganyaki, the large territory after which the lake that Goodall and Vanne traveled to was named.

The region had long been of interest to Europeans. In the late 1400s, the Portuguese landed in east Africa and controlled the area until **Oman** took control in the late 1800s. The German missionary Johannes Rebmann became the first European to see Mount Kilimanjaro in 1848.

European explorers made it to Lake Tanganyika in 1857, one hundred and three years before Goodall and her mother would arrive. German colonists began to settle in the 1880s. After World War I ended, as part of the **Treaty of Versailles,** Germany gave up all overseas territories and Britain took command of the region, renaming it the Tanganyiki Territory.

In 1947, the region became a United Nations trust territory, meaning that British settlers began arriving. There were evident class differences between the native people and European settlers. While native Africans held positions in government, many lived as subsistence farmers. Settlers from the Middle East were often merchants and white European settlers tended to own and manage farms and businesses.

Through many political events, the region would eventually declare independence from Britain in 1961. In 1964, the region united with the island of Zanzibar to form the United Republic of Tanzania.

THE ATROCITIES OF WAR

The Holocaust, a word derived from Greek that refers to a sacrificial altar, is now used to refer to the **genocide** of six million Jewish people and other ethnic and political groups by the German Nazis during World War II. While these groups faced discrimination and persecution in pre-war Germany, with many fleeing their homes, it was the concentration camps, or Hitler's so-called "final solution," that dealt the most tragic blows to the Jewish community.

While initially, the Nazis attempted to keep the operations of these camps secret, reports would soon filter back to the Allied countries as troops discovered death camps like Auschwitz, where millions of people were murdered or died of starvation.

The war, and particularly the images of the Holocaust, had a profound effect on Jane. She would later write,

[By] the time I was seven I was used to news of battles, of defeats and of victories ... Knowledge of man's inhumanity to man became more real as the newspapers and radio hinted at unspeakable horrors perpetrated on the Jews of Europe and the cruelties of Hitler's Nazi regime. Although my own life was still filled with love and security, I was slowly becoming aware of another kind of world altogether, a harsh and bitter world of pain and death and human cruelty. And although we were among the luckiest, far away from the horror of massive bombings, nevertheless, signs of war were all around … All the evil aspects of human nature had been given free rein, all the values I had been taught—the values of kindness and decency and love—had been disregarded. I can remember wondering if it was really true—how could human beings do such unspeakable things to other human beings?

Conflict in Congo

When Goodall and Vanne arrived in Kigoma in the Tanganyiki province in 1960, they arrived just as violence erupted in the area. Just a week earlier, Congo-Léopoldville, today known as the Democratic Republic of Congo, declared independence from Belgium. The Force Publique, a military first created by a Belgian king in 1885, rallied against Belgian officers and the new prime minister, Patrice Lumumba, dismissed all Belgians employed in the government. Belgians feared for their lives and fled across the river to the neighboring British territory, Tanganyiki.

The district commissioner informed the Goodall women that their trip was delayed, as the British officials in the region feared that the violence would soon spread into their region. When they returned to their hotel, Goodall and her mother were met with hundreds of Belgian refugees. They would spend the next few days greeting refugees and handing out food and supplies. Permission to head for Gombe would not be given until July 14.

ENVIRONMENTALISM

The political situation in and around Kenya and Tanzania was not the only backdrop that would inform Goodall's career. As she continued her work throughout the following decades, the public became more aware of the effects of air and water pollution, pesticides, radiation, and the finite amount of nonrenewable resources. Rachel Carson's book *Silent Spring*, published in 1962, revealed the harmful effects of farmers' pesticide use on surrounding ecosystems. Simultaneously, animal rights activists directly compared the women's liberation movement, which fought for equal pay and sexual harassment protection, to protecting animals. As the movement gained public figures and celebrity support, it became more mainstream. The environmental and animal rights movements would play a pivotal role in Goodall's future career.

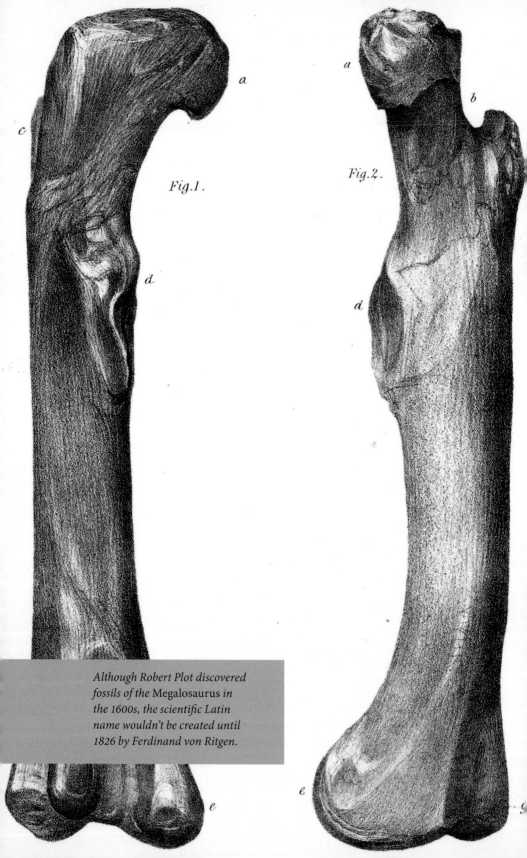

Fig.1.

Fig.2.

Although Robert Plot discovered fossils of the Megalosaurus in the 1600s, the scientific Latin name wouldn't be created until 1826 by Ferdinand von Ritgen.

CHAPTER THREE

JANE GOODALL'S FIELD OF STUDY

Goodall's beloved Gombe Reserve is settled in the midst of the Eastern African Rift Valley. A **rift** is a large fracture between continental plates that widens over time. The Earth's **lithosphere,** composed of the upper mantle and outer, rocky crust, is broken into tectonic plates. These plates move across the mantle because **convection** occurs in the second layer of the Earth. Hot material near the Earth's core rises, and cooler material sinks. This process causes Earth's tectonic plates to push together and spread apart at ridges in the ocean.

A rift valley occurs as a result of plate movement; it is one of the first stages in continental shifts. Rift valleys typically have a valley floor with large, surrounding plateaus. One of the best examples of a rift valley is the East African Rift (EAR), which extends north to south from Ethiopia to Mozambique. The rift began developing 22 to 25 million years ago as the African plate slowly split into two smaller plates. Together the EAR, along with its complement, the West African Rift, are called the Great Rift. This geographical feature can be seen from space!

Within the rift are several unique ecosystems, including the Serengeti ecosystem that extends 12,000 square miles from northern Tanzania to southern Kenya. Home to the largest land mammal migration in the world, named the Serengeti migration, this ecosystem is one of the Seven Natural Wonders of Africa. There are a number of diverse habitats within the ecosystem, including plains, swamps, and woodlands, which provide homes to over fifty large mammal species including lions, zebras, buffalo, and wildebeests.

The Serengeti migration occurs in the grass plains where herds arrive to feed between November and December of every year. When they have exhausted the resources in the area, wildebeests, zebra, and gazelle, among other species, make the 500-mile journey north to find fresh grass and water from January to March. As herds make their way through the lush, blooming grasslands, many animals die as crocodiles and other predators take advantage of the large numbers of prey.

In addition to great diversity among animal species, this region of the world is also responsible for some of the earliest known human ancestors. The EAR is also home to the Maasai tribe, who are nomadic hunters and farmers and travel around southern Kenya and northern Tanzania.

Found within the Serengeti plains, the Olduvai Gorge is a dry valley in northern Tanzania. The name derived from a Maasai word that means "the place where land moves on forever." As European settlers began visiting and inhabiting eastern Africa, a German entomologist, or insect scientist, happened upon the valley while on an expedition to collect butterflies in 1911. Along with butterfly specimens, Wilhelm Kattwinkel took several fossilized teeth, belonging to the ancient horse ancestor *Hipparion,* back with him to Germany. European scientists quickly grew excited at the possibility of more fossils and a German geologist named Hans Reck organized an official expedition to the valley in 1913. Reck and his team found several fossils and stone tools that roused the interest of none other than the famous paleoanthropologist Louis Leakey.

FOSSILS AND THE HISTORY OF HUMANKIND

The Latin word *fossus* originally meant any object that was dug from the ground. From before medieval times, humans loved to pick up interesting things from the soil and speculate on their origins. In 1546, Georgius Agricola, a Renaissance physician, wrote the book *De Natura Fossilum* (On the Nature of Fossils). Agricola described minerals, gemstones, and even some objects that would today be classified as true fossils. The book established the principles of the field of paleontology, a varied discipline that uses fossils to study the history and evolution of organisms from microbes, to plants, to invertebrates, and mammals. *De Natura Fossilum* was the first known attempt to categorize objects according to rules. Additionally, Agricola included many illustrations of his findings. Other Renaissance scientists and writers, including Leonardo de Vinci, speculated on the origin of fossils. At the time, it was not commonly believed that fossils came from living organisms; instead, prominent academics argued that either nature was simply great at creating rocks that resembled creatures or that fossils "grew" in rocks.

Robert Plot, the University of Oxford's first professor of chemistry in the late 1600s, was among the scientists of the day who believed that fossils were simply chemical formations in rocks. However, when digging in a quarry, Plot stumbled upon large bones and teeth in the rock. He identified one of the bones as a femur, or thighbone, of some unknown animal. In fact, Plot had found part of a *Megalosaurus* skeleton, a carnivorous dinosaur that lived over 190 million years ago.

After Plot's discovery, fossils continued to be collected all over Europe, and public opinion gradually accepted that fossils came from ancient living things. However, the concept of extinction was very much a theory and not a widespread belief.

George Cuvier worked as a curator at the French National Museum of Natural History in the late 1700s. The museum had a vast collection of **vertebrate** skeletons, and Cuvier set about sorting them. Shortly after he began the monumental task, the museum received a twelve-foot-high, six-foot-long skeleton from Spain. Comparing the fossilized skeleton to living animals, he concluded that the creature must have been an ancestor of the three-toed sloth, calling the creature *Megatherium fossile*. Cuvier later would give a talk titled "On the Species of Living and Fossil Elephants" in 1796, arguing that fossils found throughout Europe were the ancestors of modern-day elephants. In addition to his *M. fossile* discovery, Cuvier would go on to identify twelve other species from the museum's fossil stores including a cave bear, an ancient rhinoceros, and a mammoth skeleton. In 1815, he argued that fossils not only indicated extinction was a naturally occurring phenomenon, but that because older strata of rock did not contain fossils and that fossils from different eras were at different stages of complexity, that life had not always existed. In his lifetime, Cuvier identified over forty-eight extinct species. He did not, however, believe that humans coexisted with the organisms that he identified and pointed to the lack of human skeleton discoveries as evidence.

Another important discovery would soon shake this belief, however. The Neander Valley in western Germany was a rocky and strange landscape full of cliffs, valleys, and caves. In the mid-nineteenth century, the area was heavily mined for limestone as a result of the growing industrialization of surrounding areas. In August 1856, two workers preparing a cave for an excavation found some bones among the dirt and debris on the floor. Sixteen bones in total were discovered. The skull was different from any known human cranium at the time. The sloping forehead and protruding eyebrow ridges prompted the quarry owners to send the bones to Hermann Schaffhausen, a professor of anatomy at the University of Bonn. Schaffhausen was convinced that the bones came from an ancient type of human. He named the hypothetical ancestor the "Neanderthal man," sparking an entirely new field of study concerned with human evolution.

Another scientist, Charles Darwin, rocked the scientific world with the publication of his book *The Origin of the Species* in 1859. In it, Darwin argued that species transformed over time through the process of **natural selection.** Organisms with favorable traits that helped them survive were able to reproduce and pass on their genes. Those with less adaptive traits died and, sometimes, entire species became extinct. Other times, organisms could develop into an entirely new species with unique traits.

Meanwhile, debates over the origin of the Neanderthal man continued. Some believed the skeleton belonged to a more recently deceased human; others said that it was indeed a precursor to modern humans. Paleontologists Marcellin Boule and Elliot Smith argued that the Neanderthal man was a descendent of apes and was not related to modern humans. Other scientists, like Rudolf Virchow, believed the skeleton to belong to a modern human that was unrelated to apes. Still others, like Ales Hrdlicka, maintained that Neanderthals were simply a phase of human evolution.

By 1954, more discoveries of pre-human skeletons across Europe prompted scientists like Henri Vallois to argue that Neanderthals were in fact a separate species that lived at the same time as modern-day human ancestors. As more and more evidence was collected, particularly in Africa, Gunter Brauer, a professor at the German University of Hamburg, formulated the Afro-European sapiens hypothesis.

Early human populations, Brauer argued, migrated from Africa around 700,000 years ago to Europe. Neanderthals and modern human ancestors evolved from these early humans. Scientists Vincent Sarich and Allan Wilson applied newly discovered information about DNA, the genetic blueprint of all living things, and were able to trace the timescale of when apes and humans diverged, or split apart to become separate species, to five million years ago. Brauer's theory was now supported by actual genetic evidence.

Raymond Dart became a pivotal figure in paleoanthropology in 1924 when one of his anatomy students, a young woman named Josephine Salmons, casually mentioned that her friend had a skull of a new baboon species. Upon studying the skull, Dart noticed that the specimen had some distinct differences from modern chimpanzee and gorilla skulls. Two particular characteristics stood out. First, the teeth resembled human teeth much more than ape teeth. Secondly, the position of the foramen magnum, a hole at the base of skull through which the spinal cord passes, suggested to Dart that this particular creature walked upright like humans. He named the specimen *Australopithecus africanus* as it was the first known specimen of its kind. The young scientist quickly became a celebrity. He maintained that *A. africanus* was a direct ancestor of modern day humans.

Later studies of the specimen indicated that *A. africanus* retained the capability to climb trees while standing on two legs to eat. The species most likely ate fruit and leaves and slept in trees when available.

Louis Leakey, a contemporary of Dart's, admired him as a scientist but did not agree with his assertion of human ancestry. Leakey, instead, thought that the split between apes and humans occurred around twenty million years ago and that there were many subsequent splits after that. He theorized that *Australopithecus*, the Neanderthal man, and other discoveries were all examples of humanlike but separate species that ended in extinction. Furthermore, he believed that while these organisms may have existed at the same time as modern humans' ancestors, they had no direct effect on human evolution.

On his expedition to Olduvai, Hans Reck discovered another skeleton; when Reck announced the discovery, he pointed to both the human and ape-like features of his find. Leakey, however, believed that Reck's Olduvai skeleton was younger than his counterpart thought. When he searched the area for tools that would provide some clues to the skeleton's true age, however, Leakey's team could not find any. He would eventually concede to Reck's beliefs that the skeleton was much older. The expedition in 1931 and another in 1935 unearthed over thirty promising dig sites in Olduvai. As Leakey gained access to more robust funding, he began to conduct deeper excavations at two particular sites. At one, he and his wife found over two thousand stone tools along with many mammalian and plant fossils.

During the 1950s, while Leakey and other scientists continued to unearth clues to the evolution and development of humans, a team at the University of California, Berkeley, was working on a method to determine the age of such artifacts. Up until this point, paleontologists

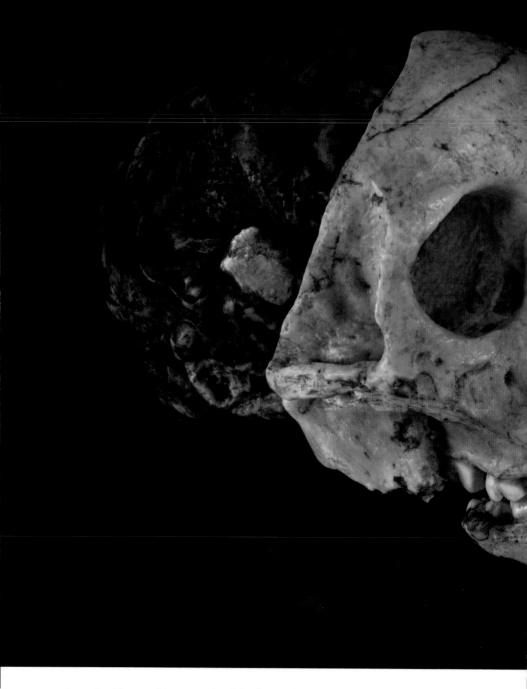

Australopithecus africanus is the oldest known human ancestor from southern Africa, but scientists still have questions about its ancestors and origins.

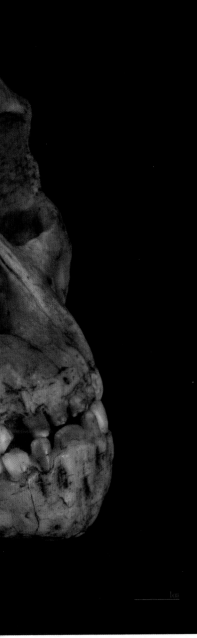

used geological clues surrounding fossils and other artifacts to estimate age. The physicists and geologists at Berkeley knew that the atoms of certain chemical elements broke down over time. As the process occurs, **radioactivity** is released, forming different chemical elements until stability is reached. For instance, the element uranium becomes lead over a long period of time. If the scientists could measure the amount of stable and unstable materials within elements, they could then determine how long ago elements were formed and thus reveal a more precise age of the rock from which they came. Several elements, such as uranium, proved to be unhelpful as the breakdown process occurred very slowly over a staggering amount of time. The Berkley group eventually would develop a **spectrometer** capable of measuring the decay rate of potassium, with just billionths of a gram of the element within a sample. Potassium-argon dating would become a foundational tool in the field of paleoanthropology.

Meanwhile, Louis Leakey sought funding from the National Geographic Society and, upon receiving a grant of over $20,000, arranged an expedition just across the Ethiopian border from Kenya in fossil beds along the Omo River. The expedition involved archeologists, anatomists, geologists, and paleontologists who, Leakey believed, would form the best and most capable team to analyze any **hominid** fossils found. As the Omo River Expedition got underway, work continued in the Olduvai valley. Leakey's nineteen-year-old son, Jonathan, assisted at his father's dig after finishing school. One day, as he ventured away from the main excavation sites, he saw a jawbone sticking out of the ground. Identifying it as a mandible that once belonged to a saber-toothed tiger, Jonathan began searching the area for more of the skeleton. While his examination did not yield any more of the extinct feline, he did find a human-like tooth and finger bone. Upon setting up the site for further digging, Jonathan found a collarbone and several skull fragments. Eventually, he would discover twelve foot bones, twenty-one hand bones, and one toe bone. These findings were scattered throughout the dig site and mixed in among the fossils of other non-human creatures. Upon examination, Leakey believed that the bones and their similarity to other human ancestors were from the oldest known human ancestor yet. He gave it the name *Homo habilis* and officially announced the discovery in 1964. The new species was added to the **genus** *Homo* along with modern-day humans, *Homo sapiens,* and another human ancestor, *Homo erectus.* The most distinguishing feature of the *Homo* genus is its large brain size, particularly in relation to body size.

Considerable debate surrounded the discovery; some scientists argued that *H. habilis* was a more advanced version of Dart's *Australopithecus africanus.* Others believed it represented a less evolved but separate genus of organisms that were ancestors of modern day *Homo sapiens.* Subsequent fossil discoveries would indicate that hominid-like species began evolving over three million years ago. *Homo*

Homo habilis *had a larger brain than the earlier* A. africanus *together with smaller face and teeth. It is thought to be the first human ancestor to use tools, thus its name, which means "handy man."*

habilis, then, acted as a middle point in human evolution as a hominid ancestor that walked upright and used tools, but also still climbed trees, approximately 1.8 million years ago.

PRIMATOLOGY

Primates are mammals that evolved from ancestors that inhabited trees. Many species today remain **arboreal**, or tree dwelling. Primates inhabit multiple ecosystems, but many live in the subtropical and jungle regions near the equator. They range in size from the mouse lemur, which weighs around 1 ounce, to the eastern gorilla, which weighs over 440 pounds! They also move in a variety of ways; various primates walk on all fours, two legs, or on their knuckles. Others leap from tree to tree or swing between branches. Primates are characterized by large brain size in comparison to body mass, and many have opposable thumbs and prehensile, or grasping, tails. Another characteristic is prehensile hands and feet, no claws, and eyes located on the front of the skull. Some primates even have color vision as a tool to collect important information about their environment. They tend to rely less on their sense of smell than other mammalian species do. Primates develop more slowly **in utero** than many other mammals and tend to have longer lifetimes. Some primate species live in large groups; others are solitary or may travel with a small group. Most are highly social and learn behaviors through observation and problem solving.

Apes were first introduced to Europeans in 1640 when a chimp was brought to the Dutch king Prince William of Orange's court. The word chimpanzee would not appear until 1738, when an article in *London Magazine* stated: "A most surprising creature is brought over … she is the female of the creature which the Angolans call chimpanzee, or mockman." Chimps and other apes would become popular attractions in European zoos but oftentimes died very early, as little was understood about their diets or habitats.

After Charles Darwin published *On The Origin of the Species,* the scientific community grew more interested in studying animal evolution, behavior, and anatomy. Early scientists like Thomas Huxley explored primatology, the study of primate anatomy and evolution. In his 1863 book, *Man's Place in Nature,* Huxley attempted to theorize about the origin of humankind. A German primatologist, Ernst Haeckel, published an encyclopedia of primate anatomy. Although the scientific community desired to learn more about humans' close relatives, not all went about their research using sound or replicable methods.

R.L. Garner, for instance, studied chimpanzees in West Africa from a cage and, upon his return to England, made exaggerated claims about the primates' intelligence. Victor Meunier, a French scientist, wrote a proposal in 1896 that called for apes and monkeys to be trained to serve food and clean people's homes.

Wolfgang Kohler produced more reliable work in the early 1900s when he studied chimpanzees on the Canary Islands. His goal was to compare and contrast the thought processes of chimps and humans. In one particular test, Kohler hung bananas from the roof of his research station; he would observe chimps developing advanced problem solving strategies to retrieve the tasty fruits. Kohler published a seminal work, *The Mentality of Apes,* in 1925, detailing his findings.

A contemporary of Kohler, Nadie Kohts, acquired a female chimp named Ioni around the same time. Kohts showed that chimps had color vision by training Ioni to match colored swatches of cloth. Ioni also could match shapes and sizes.

In 1925, Robert Yerkes, an American psychologist, began a chimpanzee colony at the Yale Laboratories of Primate Biology. Through observations in the lab setting, Yerkes collected a great deal of useful scientific information on chimpanzee behavior. However, Yerkes wanted to observe chimp behavior outside of a lab setting. A colleague of his, Winthrop Kellogg, brought home a young chimpanzee named Gua; Kellogg and his wife recorded the daily activities of both the new addition and their infant son David who was about Gua's age. In the beginning, both the young boy and the chimp performed about the same on various tasks. However, in later months, David began to outperform Gua. She could communicate nonverbally and seemed to understand some spoken English, but much to the disappointment of her adopted family, never mastered spoken language. Yerkes would continue to advocate for the study of primates, particularly chimpanzees. In 1943, he wrote,

> **❝** *The study of other primates may prove the most direct and economical route to profitable knowledge of ourselves, because, in them, basic mechanisms are less obscured by cultural influence. Certainly it is unwise to assume that human biology can be advanced only by the study of man himself. This could be true only if he existed as a unique organism, lacking genetic relations to other types of creatures.* **❞**

One of Yerkes's most famous experiments involved chimpanzee perception of color, size, and shape. The scientist would place a chimp in the middle of a room with a series of similarly sized boxes in each corner. Each box was a different shape. The chimp would observe food being placed under one box. Subsequent tests would obscure the chimp's vision as food was placed under a different box. Over time, the chimps would learn to use other clues, rather than just visual cues, to locate their breakfast.

Sherwood Washburn also played a pivotal role in transforming primate and anthropological studies. He wrote in 1951 that the study of human evolution required experts from multiple fields because evolution itself was complex and multifaceted. "[We] must collaborate with social scientists, geneticists, anatomists, and paleontologists," he wrote. "We need new ideas, new methods, new workers. There is nothing we do today which will not be done better tomorrow."

Washburn began his career by dissecting primates; however, when he observed living baboons while at the 1955 Pan-African Congress, he excitedly wrote a letter to a colleague proclaiming:

> *I see now that an entirely new level of primate behavior description is possible, one which recognizes both the generalities about the species and individual peculiarity. This would take a full year in the field to do for baboons, as getting to know one of the big, wild troops would be a significant task. However, I've learned so much on obvious things such as locomotion that I can't believe the literature contains the statements it does.*

Unfortunately, Washburn and his students would realize that baboons are not particularly good representatives of primates and that multiple long studies were needed to truly understand the complexity of primate evolution.

JANE GOODALL'S STUDIES

Goodall began her fieldwork by accompanying the Leakeys to Olduvai where she helped search for fossils. The area was so remote that, on the way there, she and another research assistant had to perch atop the expedition's Range Rover to look for old tire tracks for the driver to follow. In addition to his paleoanthropological interests, Louis also had a great interest in setting up a research project amongst apes. He was particularly interested in the mountain-dwelling chimps that lived in the area on the shore of Lake Tanganyika six hundred miles from Olduvai.

While Leakey began looking for funding for Goodall, the young scientist began to familiarize herself with the current state of primatology. When she and her mother returned to Kenya in 1960, they were met with bad news. A dispute with local fishermen in the Gombe Reserve would delay the expedition. Leakey instead sent the two to Loliu Island on Lake Victoria. Goodall would spend the next three months observing the vervet monkeys that roamed the small, 9-square-mile (14.5 square kilometer) grass-covered island.

Goodall spent her days carefully observing and recording notes. Vervets are medium-sized monkeys that weigh up to 17 pounds (7.7 kilograms); they most often inhabit woodlands surrounding lakes and rivers and spend the majority of their lives in trees. When Leakey radioed the pair about a month later to report that the Gombe dispute had been resolved, Goodall was relieved. The presence of crocodile poachers on the island created a tense atmosphere. Despite the challenges, Leakey was quite impressed with her vervet field notes. He praised her eye for detail and diligent writing.

When Vanne and Goodall arrived at Gombe in July 1960, there still existed little observational evidence of chimpanzees' behavior in the wild. For the first ten days in her new home, Jane struggled to get close to troops of chimpanzees. Each time, the chimps would run away before she could settle and begin taking notes. She was, however, able to begin adapting to the jungle's intensity. Soon, the almost constant presence of insects did not bother her, and her skin grew tougher. As she spent more time climbing the mountainous terrain, her stamina improved. Three months would pass, though, before she had a breakthrough. That morning, Goodall set off before dawn as usual. She hiked about 1,000 feet (304 m) above her camp in Kasakela Valley. As usual, she began scouting for chimps using her binoculars. Suddenly, she heard a rustling about 24 feet (8 yards) from where she sat. Turning, she was met with three curious chimps watching her. After a moment, they turned and calmly moved back into the brush. Jane quietly and eagerly waited. Her patience was finally rewarded. Several groups of chimpanzees noisily broke through the brush to a fig tree just below her perch. They spent time eating figs and drinking water before leaving. As their silent observer hurriedly took notes, the chimps were unbothered.

Goodall continued to rise at dawn and would spend most of her days crawling through dirt and brush to the spot where she first saw the chimp troop, which she referred to as the Peak. Despite the many cuts and bruises she acquired, and the daily exhaustion of climbing, she was most often rewarded with a visit from the chimpanzees. In September, she passed the previous record of sixty-four days in the field set by a predecessor in 1930.

Eventually, Goodall learned that she was observing a large group of about fifty members. She named them the Kasakela group and began to give the members names including Goliath, David Greybeard, and

Flo. Each had a unique personality and appearance. Flo, for instance, was an older female chimp with ragtag ears and a large, squished nose. Goliath was named for his immense size and David Greybeard for his thick, white beard. It was Greybeard, in fact, that provided Goodall with evidence not only that the Gombe study was important, but also that the field of primatology would be changed forever.

TOOLS AND MEAT

In October 1960, Goodall made a major discovery. As she watched a group of chimps, including David Greybeard, on the Peak, she noticed the male chimp chew something and then give it to a female and baby near him. Much to Goodall's surprise, David Greybeard was eating meat from a bush piglet. This observation was important, as up until that moment, scientists believed that chimpanzees were vegetarians. Goodall's careful observations, however, showed that chimps ate meat and were in fact omnivorous, like humans.

However, the remarkable intelligence of chimps was irrefutably proven on the morning of Friday, November 4. Goodall was, as usual, in the mountains, following the sounds of chimp cries and yells. She passed a termite mound, and when she saw that a chimp was sitting near it, she immediately dropped to the ground and scrambled to a tree for cover. She watched the chimp, who she would later identify as David Greybeard, picking things up from the ground and putting them in his mouth. But, then, remarkably, "he pulled a thick grass stalk towards him and broke off a piece about 18 inches long … It was held in the left hand, poked into the ground, and then removed coated with termites. The straw was then raised to the mouth and insects picked off with the lips, along the length of the straw, starting in the middle," Goodall wrote in her field journal.

When she sent Leakey a report of her observations, her delighted mentor wrote back, "Now we must redefine 'tool,' redefine 'man' or accept chimpanzees as humans." Leakey's excitement was justified; never before had scientists observed animals using tools. Until Goodall's

Chimpanzees have also been observed using rocks to crack nuts in addition to fishing for termites and ants.

REASON FOR HOPE

Jane reflected on her experience at Gombe in her 1999 book *Reason for Hope: A Spiritual Journey*:

I became totally absorbed into this forest existence. It was an unparalleled period when aloneness was a way of life; a perfect opportunity, it might seem, for meditating on the meaning of existence and my role in it all. But I was far too busy learning about the chimpanzees' lives to worry about the meaning of my own. I had gone to Gombe to accomplish a specific goal, not to pursue my early preoccupation with philosophy and religion. Nevertheless, those months at Gombe helped to shape the person I am today—I would have been insensitive indeed if the wonder and the endless fascination of my new world had not had a major impact on my thinking. All the time I was getting closer to animals and nature, and as a result, closer to myself and more and more in tune with the spiritual power that I felt all around. For those who have experienced the joy of being alone with nature there is really little need for me to say much more; for those who have not, no words of mine can ever describe the powerful, almost mystical knowledge of beauty and eternity that come, suddenly, and all unexpected.

Other organisms, such as corvids (crows, ravens, and rooks), otters, fish, and octopuses, have been observed using tools in the wild to obtain food and build shelter.

remarkable discovery, scientists believed that only humans were capable of that level of planning. David Greybeard and the termites he hoped to eat would catapult Goodall into a new world of both scientific respect and accolades, but also controversy and criticism.

Although it took many months, the Gombe chimpanzees soon became accustomed to, and even comfortable, around Goodall.

CHAPTER FOUR

CONTEMPORARIES, CRITICISMS, AND CONTROVERSIES

Shortly before her breakthrough discoveries, Goodall received a prestigious visitor. It was a timely visit, as Goodall was beginning to grow worried that she would not be able to secure funding to remain at Gombe. She needed some proof of the benefits of her work, something to distinguish her from previous primatologists.

Goodall received a telegram from Leakey informing her that he'd invited George Schaller and his wife, Kay, to visit his museum in Nairobi. George Schaller had been a graduate student at the University of Wisconsin, studying **zoology**, before becoming interested in primatology. When approached by a professor with the idea to study gorillas, Schaller began to research the history of primatology. He was dismayed by what he found. Multiple accounts of gorillas killed, either on purpose or by accident, frequented nineteenth-century accounts of the study of the largest living primates. In 1959, George and Kay accompanied Professor John Emlen and his wife Jinny to East Africa to conduct a survey of mountain gorillas. George and Kay would remain behind after the Emlens departed, setting up a research station in Albert National Park in what is now known as the Democratic Republic of Congo. Like Goodall, Schaller spent many days quietly hiking through the volcanic mountains, waiting for the gorillas to grow comfortable with his presence. He also, like Goodall, named the subjects of his observations, including Splitnose and Mrs. Greyhead. While George Schaller's work is recognized as one of the first scientific studies of apes in the wild, his research was cut short by the conflict between the Belgians and the newly emancipated Republic in 1960.

When Leakey invited the duo to Kigoma, Goodall traveled into town to meet them. George, Kay, and Jane returned to Gombe together. Goodall took her visitors to all her observation spots, but they saw no chimps during the Schallers' visit. Despite this disappointment, Jane excitedly reflected on George's advice in her field notes: "George said he thought if I could see chimps eating meat, or using a tool, a whole year's work would be justified."

With the subsequent discovery of chimpanzee tool use and carnivorousness, Leakey saw an opportunity to secure continued funding for his young protégé. During the initial months at Gombe, Vanne had worked both in organizing the camp and establishing a small clinic and overseeing medical aid to the locals. In fact, Goodall would go on to credit her mother's work with securing these positive relationships as a key element in her research success at Gombe.

However, Vanne soon decided to return to England. Easing the pain of her mother's departure, Goodall excitedly learned that the National Geographic Society (NGS) had agreed to pay $1,400 for her continued research. Founded as a club for elite explorers in the nineteenth century, the NGS was established as an official organization in 1888. Today, it is one of the largest scientific nonprofit organizations in the world. When the society agreed to fund Goodall in 1961, this was a large amount of money, worth approximately $11,000 in today's dollars. The award also marked a significant partnership for Goodall's future research. She and the NGS would have a long relationship throughout her career. As part of the new relationship, the organization wanted to document Goodall's findings, particularly those about tool use and meat eating. These discoveries were quite controversial at the time, with some scientists criticizing and questioning Goodall's data collection methods. An editor from NGS contacted Leakey, proposing that a photographer accompany Goodall on her observational trips to take photographs of her and her subjects. Leakey, at first, resisted. The task, he argued, was difficult and potentially disruptive. Photography equipment was not the sleek, modern technology known today and, while personal cameras were gaining popularity in the 1960s, a field photographer would still need to carry heavy and cumbersome equipment into the jungle. Furthermore, Louis worried that an additional person would disrupt Goodall's observations and impede further discoveries.

Finally, Goodall's mentor relented. He told NGS that they could send a photographer in the summer of 1961. In an attempt to prevent the negative consequences of a stranger in the camp, Jane and helpers at Gombe built several camouflaged structures, or "blinds," from which a photographer could take pictures unseen. At first, National Geographic suggested that Leakey send his son, Richard, but Leakey refused. Next, the organization, convinced that Goodall could simply take her own photos, sent her a complicated camera that she could not figure out how to use. Finally, at Jane's suggestion, her younger sister Judy traveled to Gombe to photograph the chimps. However, National Geographic refused this plan at first. It was only at the offer of a British newspaper to fund Judy's travel in exchange for some exclusive interviews that the plan proceeded. Weather would subsequently become the greatest barrier, and the youngest Goodall was unable to take photos until November because of frequent rainstorms in the jungle.

Cambridge

While the Goodall sisters traipsed through the jungle, Leakey was hard at work securing a place for Jane at the University of Cambridge. Founded in 1209, Cambridge is the second-oldest university in the Western world and a world-renowned academic institution.

Gaining admittance for Goodall would be particularly challenging, as she had not yet acquired her bachelor's degree. Before her attendance, only seven people obtained PhDs with no prior credentials. The Doctor of Philosophy degree, or PhD, has been awarded at European universities since the Middle Ages and requires students to submit a dissertation or book-length work of original research. Because of the demanding nature of the degree, prior university work, most often in the form of a bachelor's degree, is often a requirement.

Nevertheless, Leakey was successful. He convinced the Cambridge admissions committee that Goodall's experience in Gombe qualified her for a doctorate. On December 5, 1962, the sisters left Gombe for London. All of Judy's film was rushed to the National Geographic Society in Washington, DC. The Society received one black and white roll and twenty-three rolls of color film. Upon development, however, the NGS soundly rejected the photographs. One staffer went so far as to refer

Goodall and the Gombe chimpanzees became international sensations and were featured in magazine articles and on television. Here, she and a chimp pose for a still from the documentary Miss Goodall and the World of Chimpanzees.

to the photos as "not suitable for publication in [*National Geographic* magazine]." The sisters received a rejection letter that noted: "a lack of good pictures of the animals in the native habitat" barred the possible publication of an article featuring Jane.

Despite this setback, Goodall divided her time for the next three years between Cambridge and Gombe. She began her studies in ethology, a rapidly changing field. At the beginning of the twentieth century, ethology, or the study of animal behavior, was not a scientifically recognized discipline. Many in the scientific world regarded "naturalists" as amateurs. Ethology was first coined by Oskar Heinroth, the director of the aquarium at the Berlin Zoological Gardens, in the early twentieth century. In his categorization of European birds, Heinroth helped to combine field observations with scientific categorization. Many ethologists, including the well-known Konrad Lorenz, believed that humans should not interfere with nature. Lorenz, a Bavarian naturalist, argued that true animal behavior could only be captured through meticulous, uninvolved observation. Jane had not heard the word ethology until she began her education at Cambridge under the supervision of her advisor, Robert Hinde.

Robert Hinde worked at Cambridge's subdepartment of Animal Behavior in the small village of Madingley, just outside Cambridge. Hinde had studied ethology at Oxford University, before which he had trained as a pilot in the Royal Air Force during World War II. After serving for six years, he returned as a twenty-three-year-old undergraduate student to Cambridge. He felt uncomfortable in his classes, where he was often the oldest. In fact, he approached his mentor several times to declare his intention to quit Cambridge and become a commercial airline pilot. Hinde never went through with this plan and, instead, went on to study birds at Oxford. The study of animals eventually morphed into zoology, and he became a research professor at the University of Cambridge. As an advisor to Goodall, he at first disagreed with her unconventional research. But eventually, despite their disagreements, Hinde and Goodall would become close friends.

As Goodall continued her studies at Cambridge, she gained recognition in the scientific community. While she enjoyed studying, she longed to return to the chimps and Gombe. Her time away, however, was being well spent. Goodall presented her work and findings at two conferences, one in London and the other in New York City. Her patient method of observation and her discovery of carnivorousness and tool use among chimpanzees were exciting to primatologists, zoologists, anthropologists, and others in the scientific community. As Goodall's name became more and more known, the National Geographic Society became convinced of the importance of her story. They offered to fly her and a photographer back to Gombe in February of 1962, but both Leakey and Goodall refused. The timeline was much too short, and Goodall was not prepared to leave her studies at Cambridge yet.

SIR SOLLY AND THE CONFERENCE

Around the time that Goodall entered Cambridge to pursue her PhD, she was invited to speak at a conference on primates by Sir Solly Zuckerman, a famed primatologist and head of the Department of Anatomy at Birmingham University. Sponsored by the London Zoological Society, the conference included both seasoned scientists and academic novices like Goodall.

In her talk, Goodall revealed all the discoveries that she had made at Gombe so far. She showed pictures of David Greybeard using tools at the termite mounds. She discussed the many hours spent observing the chimps eating and her discovery that they ate meat. After speakers at the symposium had given their talks, it was customary for audience members to ask questions. However, after Goodall's talk, an audience member asked a question that directly opposed Sir Solly's previous research. Thirty years prior, he had conducted extensive research on baboons and concluded that all primates were vegetarians. When Sir Solly gave his closing speech for the day, he noted that "there are some here who prefer anecdote—and what I must confess I regard as

Goodall, pictured here with David Greybeard, welcomed the chimps into her camp and would often feed them bananas, which promoted criticism from many in the scientific world.

sometimes unbounded speculation" and reminded the audience the importance of remembering "that in scientific work it is far safer to base one's major conclusions and generalizations on a concordant and large body of data than on a few contradictory and isolated observations, the explanation of which sometimes leaves little to be desired." It was evident to the audience, and to Goodall herself, that Sir Solly was referencing Goodall's work.

Other attendees at the symposium included Alison Jolly, who studied hand use and vision in primates and how these adaptations fit in with human evolution. Goodall and Jolly formed a long friendship after this conference, and Goodall soon traveled to Yale University in New Haven, Connecticut, to visit her new friend. Jolly would go on to study lemurs in Madagascar and have a long, successful career as a famed primatologist herself.

THE BANANA CLUB

The next time Goodall left for Africa in 1963, it was without her sister or mother. She worried about her prolonged absence from the Reserve: Would the chimpanzees recognize her? Or would she be forced to start building trust from scratch? That could take months, and the prospect unsettled Goodall. Upon her arrival to camp, however, she was greeted by some happy news. In her absence, a male chimp had wandered into the camp, climbed the palm tree directly over Goodall's tent, and proceeded to eat there for about an hour. The day after her arrival, the same male came back, climbed the palm tree, ate, and then left. On his way out, he curiously peeked into Goodall's tent, interested in her return. The chimp, David Greybeard, returned to the camp each day to eat. On one particular occasion, Goodall was sorting supplies outside her tent when she noticed David Greybeard close by. He was positioned in what Goodall knew to be a posture of chimpanzee aggression or nervousness, with his hair standing on end. As she watched, the chimp lunged for a banana on a nearby table and scurried by into the safety of the jungle before eating it. Delighted by this behavior, Goodall instructed a research assistant to begin setting out bananas for the chimps each day.

David continued returning to camp and, each day, he would take a banana off the table and saunter back into the shrubs to enjoy his tasty treat. On one occasion, just after recovering from a bout of **malaria**, Goodall noticed a second visitor at the camp. As David grabbed his snack, another chimp, Goliath, waited in the bushes on the outskirts of camp. When David rejoined his friend, he spat a large wad into the other chimp's hand, and the two returned the next day. This time Goliath accompanied David into the camp to grab a banana treat. Observing from her tent, Jane was overjoyed! Here was an opportunity to study each individual chimp. She acquired a large box of bananas from a neighboring village to offer to the chimps. This became known as the Banana Club. Each day David would return to the camp, sometimes alone and sometimes with Goliath or other chimps in tow. Watching them, Goodall began to understand their unique personalities. As they grew more comfortable in camp, she decided to take the Banana Club one step further. As David entered camp one day, instead of leaving the banana out on the table, Goodall offered it to him in her hand. Although cautious at first and displaying bristled hair, David conceded and took the banana right from her hand.

The experiment did not go so well when Goodall tried it with Goliath. Goliath's hair also bristled, but he then threw a chair at Jane and charged her, almost hitting her. Then Goliath stomped back into the grass and refused bananas for some time after that.

It was through these observations and interactions that Jane was able to decipher some more details about her three main visitors, David

Greybeard, Goliath, and another chimp named William. Goliath was the dominant male. Others would back away if Goliath approached their meal; subordinate chimps would step aside when he passed, and Goliath occupied any nest he pleased. William, on the other hand, was docile and gentle. He seemed cautious and would only accept a banana from Goodall if it were placed on the ground.

David was a bit of a mystery. He seemed to be able to comfort William when he was nervous, but also consoled Goliath when he became aggressive and tense. He often was a calming force and would groom agitated group members. Over time, Goodall began to understand that each of the chimps had a distinct and unique personality. This realization countered many scientific beliefs at the time that separated humans from other animals; instead, through her observations, Jane was beginning to see that the apes were capable of friendship and **altruism.** Their interactions extended well beyond instincts and mere survival. The Gombe chimps hugged and kissed one another, decided whom to travel with each day, reasoned and problem-solved, and used tools. They also fought one another on occasion, kicking and punching. They formed friendships and grudges. Goodall was amazed at the range of behaviors she observed. Her field notes revealed her awe and gratitude for her new life. In a field report to Leakey, Goodall wrote, "The hills and forest are my home. And what is more, I think my mind works like a chimp's subconsciously."

David Greybeard was key in unlocking many of Goodall's initial discoveries. One day, as she lay beneath a fig tree observing David eating above her, she heard a great deal of rustling, and branches and twigs began falling. David climbed down and sat near Goodall for a few moments grooming himself. He also lay down and gazed up through the tree branches for a while with her. When he got up, Goodall quietly followed him to a creek where he sat near the bank. Noticing fruit lying on the ground, she picked it up and offered it to him; David reached out, took the fruit, and dropped it on the ground. He rested his hand on Goodall's for a moment. On this day, the two shared something special. Goodall felt accepted by David and understood that her presence was welcome among the troop. In the following weeks, David would act as her guide deeper into the chimps' world. Goodall recalled a moment in her notes in which she was following David. Noticing the human behind him, David let out a series of pants and hoots alerting the other chimps to both his and Goodall's presence. She was able to sit and watch the adult and young chimpanzees eating, playing, and grooming for the afternoon.

FAME, MARRIAGE, AND CRITIQUES

Although both Goodall and her mentor feared encroaching development, tourists, and other unwelcome changes to Gombe that could be caused by media attention, in 1962, the National Geographic Society sent Baron Hugo van Lawick to document Goodall's work. Van Lawick was a Dutch photographer, and Leakey had initially recommended him for the project. Goodall was cautious around the stranger, but she soon learned that they shared a common love for animals. Societal pressures for women still existed at the time, and the NGS deemed it improper for a single man and woman to work alone together in the jungle and so, once again, Vanne joined her daughter at Gombe as a chaperone. On his first visit, van Lawick stayed at Gombe for over six weeks. During that time, he captured an intense fight between David Greybeard and the other chimps and a band of baboons. To this day, van Lawick's photographs of this fight are still considered one of the best examples of documented cross-species aggression.

Goodall left Gombe for Cambridge in early 1963. While she hated to leave the chimps, she understood Leakey's insistence that she complete her studies; with a PhD, Goodall's work would be taken as more legitimate and credible by the scientific community. She worked in England until the spring, when both she and van Lawick returned to Gombe. The pair continued the Banana Club, even constructing special steel feed boxes and a protective cage in case the chimps ever became too aggressive.

Working closely together, van Lawick and Goodall soon fell in love. Van Lawick asked Goodall to marry him in December 1963 while the two were abroad for Christmas. Goodall immediately agreed, and the two were wed on March 28, 1964.

In addition to her academic studies, Goodall's reputation in scientific circles was growing. In August 1963, *National Geographic* published her first article, "My Life Among Chimpanzees." In it, she described her work in Tanganyika in vivid, exciting detail. The same year, Goodall also received the Franklin Burr Award from the National Geographic Society for her contributions to science, which came with a $1,500 stipend. This stipend would enable Jane to finalize plans to travel back to Gombe in the spring and continue research over the summer.

Toward the end of 1963 and into 1964, Goodall worked on a proposal for a research center in Gombe that could act as living quarters and a centralized base for the busy research hub. She sent the proposal to the National Geographic Society, which they approved. In December 1964, Goodall returned to Gombe to found the Gombe Stream Research Center; construction of the center was completed in 1965. By that point, students and native Tanzanians lived and worked at the reserve. Goodall hosted prominent scientists like Hans Hass, a well-known biologist, and important dignitaries like the president of Kenya. The center had

As Goodall's influence in the international community grew, she spent less and less time at Gombe but continued making field observations when her schedule allowed.

a lovely view of the lake and jungle. It consisted of a kitchen, sleeping rooms, and storage areas. Van Lawick and Goodall slept in a separate, smaller building.

The year 1965 continued to bring even more changes for the newlyweds. Jane received her PhD from Cambridge, wrote a second NGS article, "New Discoveries Among Africa's Chimpanzees," and appeared in the documentary film *Miss Goodall and the Wild*

Chimpanzees, which premiered on American television and propelled her to international recognition.

Despite her growing reputation, however, not everyone was receptive or supportive of her research methods. In fact, her own advisor at Cambridge, Dr. Hinde, criticized her for "humanizing" the chimps by assigning them names as opposed to the traditional approach of identifying animal subjects with numbers. He was so opposed to Goodall's names that in the first copy of her **thesis,** Hinde marked out all gender pronouns and replaced them with "it." When she received the manuscript with his edits, Goodall heatedly changed all the revisions back to "him" and "her." She also kept the chimpanzees' names. Unfortunately, Hinde was not Goodall's only critic. Other ethologists criticized her for anthropomorphizing the chimps' behavior. To anthropomorphize means to attribute human personality characteristics to an animal's behavior. By naming the chimps, other ethologists believed that Goodall's research was not objective and was too influenced by emotions. However, she defended her work then and has continued to do so throughout her life. In a 2010 interview with *Scientific American*, Goodall explained,

> ❝ *We're so arrogant. We think everything we do must be of a different nature and a different order of magnitude; therefore, anything that looks like human behavior in animals obviously can't possibly be anything like ours. I was criticized hugely when I first talked in 1960 about chimpanzees having emotions and feelings and being able to think. Reasoning and emotions were supposed to be unique to us, as was personality. Fortunately, as a child I'd been taught by my dog Rusty that that wasn't*

true. Animals have moods—they can sulk, they can be happy, they can be sad. I knew Rusty could think, I knew he could work out problems. And he definitely had a very distinct personality, different from any other dog I've ever had. So even if you go way down the evolutionary scale, you find quite different personalities between members of the same group. Yet when I first talked about individual differences among the chimps, I was told by ethologists that, 'Well, yes, maybe there are such things, but we don't really understand them, so we shouldn't talk about them.' **"**

Other critics voiced concerns that the Banana Club altered the chimpanzees' natural feeding and social behavior. In her observations of the chimps at the camps, Goodall noted aggressive behavior. Her critics speculated on whether this was an accurate representation of wild chimpanzee behavior or if the presence of large quantities of free bananas affected their interactions. However, later studies would show that the banana feeding did not substantially change the chimps' behaviors, as similar activity was subsequently observed among other chimpanzee groups without access to provisions.

Lastly, Goodall would continue to be criticized as a female scientist throughout her life. When her first article was published in *National Geographic*, several peers scoffed at the idea of a young, blonde woman on the cover. Goodall continued to produce scientifically valid and legitimate research to disprove the negative stereotypes that she encountered. As she published more articles and became more publicly recognized, she also drew criticism from women's liberation activists. While Goodall embodied characteristics of independence and intelligence, some Second Wave feminists criticized her for promoting traditional gender roles among the chimpanzees.

THE KIDNAPPING

In addition to the criticism that accompanied Goodall's career, she also dealt with the danger of doing research in a tumultuous and often unstable area. In 1975, almost a decade after the Gombe Research Center was constructed, rebels from Zaire, now known as the Democratic Republic of the Congo, crossed Lake Tanganyika and raided the reserve. Hoping to raise funds to fuel their revolutionary mission to overthrow the government in Zaire, the rebels kidnapped four students living at Gombe at the time, three Americans and one Dutch. Several weeks passed with no word, and the government ordered all foreigners at the Research Center to leave. Goodall and the other staff members waited anxiously in Dar es Salaam, Tanzania. After several excruciating weeks, one of the students showed up with a ransom note. The kidnappers' demands were extreme, both in the amount of money demanded and what was expected from the Tanzanian government. Finally, two rebels traveled to the city to negotiate with the American and Dutch **embassies.** Despite the ransom being paid, the kidnappers initially returned two more of the hostages but kept the last in captivity. All feared for the hostage's life, but he was finally released. After this, the Tanzanian government declared Gombe to be a "sensitive" area; visitors were required to have a special security clearance and students would not return to the center until 1989.

At the time, Goodall was teaching at Stanford University in California. After the kidnapping incident, criticism and rumors flew. Some argued that Goodall should have volunteered in the students' stead; others claimed that she did not do enough to ensure their safe return. For a time, Goodall was even advised to take a leave of absence from her professor duties at Stanford, but she refused.

THE FOUR YEARS WAR

In the early 1970s, Goodall observed a major shift in the chimp community. The group had divided into two, with the Kasakela group remaining in the valley where Jane first observed them, and

SIR SOLLY ZUCKERMAN

Solly Zuckerman was an early and important primatologist. Born in Cape Town, South Africa, Zuckerman studied anatomy under Raymond Dart at Cape Town University. He became a research anatomist at the London Zoo where he dissected deceased zoo animals. There, he also observed the behavior of baboons in captivity. These observations, coupled with field observations in South Africa, led Zuckerman to develop a profound theory in 1932. He postulated that primates were held together socially by males fighting one another for dominance and females. Zuckerman would become highly successful, eventually becoming chair of the Department of Anatomy at Birmingham University in England and the chief scientific advisor to the military during World War II. As a result of his service, Zuckerman became quite influential in the scientific world. He would become knighted and was thereafter known as Sir Solly Zuckerman.

a second group forming and moving south. She named this group Kahama. From 1974 to 1978, Jane saw terrible acts of violence against the Kahama group by the Kasakelas. Male Kasakela chimps would attack rival males in the other group, often biting, hitting, and kicking them to death. These attacks continued until almost all the Kahama male chimps were dead. A mother-daughter pair of chimps, Passion and Pom, proceeded to systematically kill all the infants in the area except for one.

Goodall was heartbroken. All the positive traits that she had observed in the chimpanzees seemed insignificant in the light of all the violence and death. Jane wrote an article in 1979 entitled "Life and Death at Gombe" for *National Geographic* in which she detailed what she called the Four Year War. She and the magazine were criticized for the graphic and violent article along with criticisms of her observations. However, the tragic events at Gombe during that time would help to support Goodall's ideas—that individual animals had histories, temperaments, and attitudes that influenced their behavior. At a talk two years after the publication of the article, Jane reluctantly spoke at a fundraiser for Louis Leakey's Foundation entitled "Cannibalism and Warfare in Chimp Society." In her talk, she described how the mother and daughter team, only two chimps, had a profound impact on the rest of the community. Because of their actions, an entire generation of young chimps had been killed and eaten. Because of the actions of the Kasakela males, all the Kahama males were dead. The Four Year War was the first recorded incidence of warfare in nonhuman primate species. Goodall was saddened to think that the chimps' behavior resembled the violence she witnessed as a child and that the chimps' aggression could result in so much fear and trauma.

Infant chimps rely on their mothers similarly to human babies. An adolescent chimp may in fact stay with his or her mother until adulthood.

CHAPTER FIVE

JANE GOODALL'S IMPACT AND LEGACY

2010 marked the fiftieth year of research at Gombe National Park. When Goodall began, the scientific world very much believed that humans were distinctly separate from other animals. The personalities, emotions, familial bonds, and strife between different groups, it was widely believed, made *Homo sapiens* distinct and unique from any other animal group. When Goodall first journeyed to Gombe in 1960, chimpanzees filled research labs; researchers knew that their blood type and immune system functioned similar to those of humans and that many commonalities existed between chimpanzee and human brains. However, it was genuinely believed that chimps, other apes, and nonprimate species were incapable of feeling fear or sadness, so they were kept in small cages in labs across the world. Many predecessors of modern-day health and beauty products were first tested on primate subjects. Because of the research of Goodall and her contemporaries, primatology in the twenty-first century looks very different than when the shy, twenty-six-year-old English girl first pitched her tent in the wild jungle.

It is widely recognized today that chimpanzees and other primates not only have unique, individual characteristics and personalities but that, just as in humans, behaviors and proclivities are passed from parent to child through multiple generations. Research on animals other than chimps, including dolphins, wolves, and elephants, has further indicated that complex group behavior is not limited to humans. Additionally, when Goodall began her research at Gombe, developmental stages like childhood and adolescence were believed to exist only in humans; through the work at the reserve and the studies of other scientists, it is now understood that chimps also go through unique stages of growth and maturity.

Furthermore, it is now widely recognized that chimps possess positive traits, but also display aggression and conflict. After Goodall publicized the events of the Four Year War, later research indicated that the level of aggression that Goodall observed in the Gombe chimpanzees was not unique to the Kasakela and Kahama groups. Instead, tribal warfare in chimpanzees has been found in multiple regions of African. Over the course of fifty years, Goodall and her research partners at Gombe learned that aggression was the second cause of death after disease. She and her team would also learn that chimpanzees experienced not only naturally occurring diseases, like the precursor to HIV, but others, like certain respiratory illnesses, which were passed on from humans.

In 1960, ethology limited its practitioners to using notebooks, binoculars, and their analyses. Technology has since improved, and modern-day scientists observing animal behavior use computer-based analysis tools to analyze their notes. Furthermore, DNA technology has enabled scientists to document and learn more information about how chimpanzees are related. Mapping technology also allows modern-day primatologists to understand where chimp tribes live and aid in conservation efforts. Many primate tribes live near villages, and it is important that the two peacefully interact.

I OWE IT TO THE CHIMPS

When the Gombe Stream Research Center was founded in 1964, Goodall had two student researchers working with her. By the 1970s, the Center was hosting up to twenty students at a time. As of the twenty-first century, research at Gombe has expanded beyond primatology. Modern-day efforts include conservation, gender equality, habitat maintenance, science and technology, and youth engagement. The research focus has changed, in part, due to the changing political and social climates of the surrounding countries. Just as Goodall's first journey into eastern Africa was disrupted by civil unrest, conflict has consistently operated in the background of Gombe research. When Tanzania, formally Tanganyika, gained independence from the British in 1961, a new government took control. Julius Nyerere, the **socialist** leader, started the Ujamaa movement in which scattered villagers were moved into centralized farming communities. Communal farming in the 1970s resulted in significant deforestation, particularly in the area surrounding Gombe. At the same time, the 1972 Burundian genocide was occurring to the north of the reserve. Refugees fleeing the conflict hid the hills surrounding Gombe, contributing to the added human influence and habitat destruction in the area.

The Jane Goodall Institute was founded in 1977 to promote habitat conservation and youth action. According to its mission statement, the institute:

❝ *believe[s] that every individual matters and makes an impact. We are a global nonprofit committed to community-centered conservation, whether it be protecting chimpanzees and great apes in Africa while improving the lives of communities around ape habitats, or supporting youth-led efforts around the world to improve their own communities.* **❞**

Over time, research at Gombe has grown to include the villagers and refugees. In the early seventies, Tanzanian guides, first solely responsible for guiding visiting students through the mountains and valleys, began collecting their own data: observing which chimps were spending time with each other, what they were eating, and where they journeyed in a day. Goodall began offering training in Kiswahili, a common language spoken in multiple eastern countries of Africa.

In 1986, Goodall published the book *The Chimpanzees of Gombe* and attended the conference "Understanding Chimpanzees," which was, at that point, the largest gathering of chimpanzee experts in history. Researchers, scientists, students, and representatives from zoos and laboratories were all present. Each attendee was dedicated to unharmful research and had gained approval to attend based on their previous work. While the conference was held to celebrate Goodall's new book and accomplishments, it was also centered around the global plight of chimpanzees. At that point in her career, Goodall focused only on the chimps at Gombe and the problems that plagued the particular region. However, the conference opened her eyes to the horrors and dangers faced by primates all over the world. Asian primates, including gorillas, orangutans, and chimpanzees, were losing habitat space and being hunted for food. Primates in Zaire lived in a war zone and endured the consequences of a brutal civil conflict. After many presentations, thirty attendees of the conference decided to found the Committee for the Conservation and Care of Chimpanzees (CCCC), which is financed through the Jane Goodall Institute.

For Goodall, this was a revelation. She began speaking out on behalf of primates beyond Gombe's boundaries. For many years, she received criticism from animal rights groups and activists due to her apparent indifference for chimps outside of Gombe. With the success of her new book and a new, informed passion, Goodall began visiting with heads of state and politicians. She gave lectures, hosted awareness campaigns, and attended fundraisers. She appeared on many television programs promoting the cause. Goodall also worked closely with the CCCC, publishing vast amounts of information on the conditions of both captive and wild apes. She also extensively toured medical and research laboratories, often vocally speaking out about lab primates living in terrible conditions. Her efforts resulted in the United States government altering legislation, requiring labs to focus on living conditions and quality of life for animal test subjects.

In another attempt to educate the global community about conservation and animal protection efforts, Goodall founded Roots & Shoots in 1991. After observing the curiosity and passion for animals in young students hampered by a lack of resources in the community, Goodall created the program to enable young people could tackle small-scale problems in their communities and complete projects to benefit the environment, animals, and their neighbors. The group began with 12 student members and now operates in over 130 countries with over 150,000 student activists.

In 1994, as a result of the continued influx of refugees, primarily from Zaire, into the hills surrounding Gombe Reserve, the Jane Goodall

A family of chimpanzees explores a lake using tools; chimpanzees' tool use was first discovered by Jane Goodall in Gombe.

Jane Goodall: Primatologist and UN Messenger of Peace

Institute founded the TACARE ("Take Care") program to support healthy and productive lives for peoples living around and in Gombe while preventing further chimpanzee habitat destruction.

When asked how she feels about spending so much time away from Gombe, Goodall points out, "I owe it to the chimps."

MAJOR FINDINGS

Fifty years of work at Gombe has resulted in remarkable new information on chimps and, more recently, baboons. It all began, however, with Goodall's observations of David Greybeard catching termites and consuming meat. Her findings and contributions extend well beyond these two groundbreaking discoveries. Through her tireless work climbing the mountains and valleys of Gombe, Jane observed chimpanzee development, habitats, eating habits, extended tool use, and familial relationships.

Chimps travel each day in search of food. During and after a day of eating plants, ants, bird eggs, and honey, troops nap on the forest floor or make arboreal nests. Nests are constructed from tree branches and leaves to form sleeping beds. Infant chimps behave in many similar ways to human babies. They explore and play, curiously exploring their environment. Like humans, baby chimps are born helpless but can cling to their mothers with strong hands and feet. Mother chimps offer constant physical comfort and reassurance. Chimpanzee infant mortality is relatively high, so a female will raise around three babies during her lifetime. A baby chimp greatly depends on his or her mother until a sibling is born, typically every five years. While males do not interact as much with individual infants, they protect all the offspring in their group.

Although most of a chimp's diet is plant-based, groups will hunt and kill small bush pigs, monkeys, and antelope on occasion. Who gets to eat is dependent on social rank. Chimpanzee groups are highly structured with a single male most often claiming the highest rank and mating with the most females. Chimps are territorially aggressive and conflict, such as that between the Kasakela and Kahama groups, occurs both with and without provocation. A dominant male may keep his reign for up to ten years. When prey is killed by a younger, less dominant member, most often all members share. If an older, dominant male makes the kill, he decides who in the group eats. Mothers consistently share with their offspring.

About fifty members will make up a single chimpanzee community, and each member knows all the others individually. Communication occurs through calls, and each chimpanzee has a distinct voice. Chimps also use touch frequently to show affection and for intimidation. When male chimps feel threatened, all of their hair will stand up to create a larger and aggressive presence. Grooming enables group members to set up and maintain friendships and to destress.

Gombe chimpanzees use tools, primarily sticks, to catch army ants, create holes in trees to search for honey, and investigate strange objects. They will also use leaves to collect liquid and to wipe away dirt or blood. Rocks and sticks are used as weapons during conflict, and chimps in other parts of Africa have since been observed using rocks to crack open nuts that grow regionally.

Research at Gombe, in conjunction with advances in primatology and genetics, has contributed to our understanding of humans and chimpanzees' relatedness. Chimps experience emotions like fear, joy, and sadness. They are susceptible to human diseases. Gombe

Birute Galdikas continues to study and advocate for orangutans. The rainforests of Borneo and Sumatra form the great apes' only habitats and are under threat from logging and palm-oil plantations.

was struck by two severe epidemics, the first in 1966, when fifteen Kasakela chimps were infected with polio. Polio is an infectious disease that spreads orally. It causes paralysis and can eventually lead to death. In 1952, the largest epidemic in United States history affected almost 58,000 people, primarily infants and children below the age of nine. As a response, Jonas Salk invented a **vaccine**. This vaccine eliminated polio completely from North and South America by 1994. However, in Gombe in 1966, six chimps died from the epidemic, leaving the survivors disabled for the rest of their lives. In 1968, a flu-like disease again swept through the Reserve and killed two mothers. Their infants became depressed and malnourished and they, too, died. Incidents of illness exchange between humans and chimps indicate the similarity between human and chimpanzee DNA. *Homo sapien* and chimpanzee DNA differs by just 1 percent, and the two species can transfer blood if necessary.

In the late 1980s, when an outbreak of pneumonia killed eleven chimps and orphaned a young male chimp named Mel, an older male, Spindle, adopted the youngster, the first recorded observation of a nonrelated adoption. Spindle's care for Mel also indicated that male chimps were capable of nurturing and caring behavior.

THE TRIMATES

Louis Leakey acted as a great mentor and champion for Goodall's research, but she was not the only young, female scientist that he encouraged. Called the Trimates, Jane Goodall, Dian Fossey, and Biruté Galdikas are called "the founding mothers of contemporary field primatology." All three embraced living among their research subjects:

Goodall maintains a busy traveling schedule, giving lectures and interviews and meeting the young people involved in Roots & Shoots.

Goodall with the Gombe chimps, Fossey with mountain gorillas in Rwanda, and Galdikas with orangutans in Indonesia and Malaysia.

Dian Fossey was born in 1932 in San Francisco, California. Dealing with acceptance issues at home, Fossey turned to animals for comfort and companionship as a young girl. She graduated with a bachelor's degree in occupational therapy in 1954. Working at a children's hospital in Kentucky, Fossey befriended a coworker and was frequently invited to their family farm. In 1963, she used her entire life savings on a seven-week trip to Africa; while there, Fossey visited the Olduvai Gorge and met Louis and Mary Leakey. Louis Leakey described the work of Goodall, already in the field, to Fossey, as well as the continued need for primatology research. Upon returning home to Louisville, Fossey published several short articles detailing her travels. When Leakey made a stop in Kentucky on a lecture series, Fossey went to visit him and show him the writings and photographs from her visit. Recalling that the young woman had shown keen interest in mountain gorillas, Leakey set about securing funding for a project very similar to Goodall's. Fossey began her studies in the Virunga National Park in Congo in 1967, but due to civil conflict in the region, she eventually transferred her research to territory in Rwanda. Fossey went on to have a successful career; she was considered the world's foremost expert on mountain gorillas. After acquiring her PhD at Cambridge, Fossey taught as a professor at Cornell University in New York. She published the best-selling book *Gorillas in the Mist,* which was the basis for a subsequent feature film. However, before it was released, Fossey was mysteriously and tragically murdered in her cabin in Rwanda. A research assistant discovered her body in December 1985, and while several people were arrested for suspected involvement, no one has yet to serve for the crime.

AWARDS AND RECOGNITION

In her long and fruitful career, Jane Goodall has been recognized many, many times. In 1965, she graduated as the eighth recipient of a PhD with no undergraduate coursework. In the early 1970s, Goodall was appointed as a visiting professor at Stanford University in the Department of Psychiatry and Human Behavior. In 1980, she was awarded the Order of the Golden Ark and the World Wildlife Award for Conservation. Since then, she has received numerous honors. In 2002, Goodall was appointed a United Nations Messenger of Peace. Queen Elizabeth II named her a Dame Commander of the Order of the British Empire in 2004. Goodall is also internationally recognized; she has been the recipient of the Medal of Tanzania, the Japanese Kyoto Prize, the Benjamin Franklin Medal in Life Science, and the Gandhi-King Award for Nonviolence to name just a few. The Tree of Life at Disney World's Animal Kingdom features a plaque honoring Goodall and a statue of David Greybeard. Goodall holds honorary doctorate degrees from eight different universities and has received an award or recognition almost every year of her career since 1980.

By the mid-1990s, Goodall was traveling approximately 300 days a year, giving lectures, appearing on programs, and visiting zoos, research institutes, and laboratories. Although she realized that her actions were necessary for publicity for the chimps' plight, she would often think of Gombe and the first few years roaming the jungle, interacting with David Greybeard, and the excitement of discovery.

PRIMATOLOGY RESEARCH TODAY

Today, primatology continues to advance at the Gombe Stream Research Center. The Center still promotes citizen science, conservation efforts, and training Tanzanian researchers. Because Goodall's research laid the

UNITED NATIONS MESSENGER OF PEACE

The United Nations Messenger of Peace is awarded to "distinguished individuals, carefully selected from the fields of art, literature, science, entertainment, sports or other fields of public life, who have agreed to help focus worldwide attention on the work of the United Nations." Designees are recognized for their humanitarian efforts and work as global citizens, improving the lives of people in many countries. After appointment, UN Messengers of Peace attend special fundraising concerts, speak at United Nations events, and advocate for different campaigns. As of 2016, there were thirteen Messengers including actor Leonardo DiCaprio, world-renowned violinist Yo-Yo Ma, Holocaust survivor and author Elie Wiesel, musician Stevie Wonder, and Jane Goodall.

Appointed as a UN Messenger of Peace in 2002, Jane speaks about the United Nations' conservation campaigns. The organization, consisting of many different country members, addresses many different areas of environmentalism including climate change, sustainable energy, soil erosion, and pollution prevention.

Upon being presented with the distinguished title by then Secretary-General Kofi Annan, Jane said, "It is an honor to be appointed a United Nations Messenger of Peace by the Secretary-General. I will pledge to take the new responsibility very seriously. I shall attempt to carry the appropriate message as I travel around the world."

foundation for understanding chimpanzee behaviors and similarities to humans, Gombe research turns now to the field of epidemiology and immunology. Gombe chimps are now so used to humans, scientists can observe and collect samples at close distances. Sample collection, particularly of urine and feces, is necessary for Dr. Beatrice Hahn's research in particular. Hahn first founded a lab at the University of Alabama-Birmingham where she studied the origins of human immunodeficiency virus (HIV) and Acquired Immunodeficiency Syndrome (AIDS). HIV attacks a person's immune system, killing off defensive cells, and increasing risk of infection. As of 2016, there is no cure for HIV, but several medications have been developed that, when taken consistently, can keep an individual's immune system healthy and functioning. Globally, the disease is very widespread. In 2014, it was estimated that 36.9 million people were living with the disease. While HIV and AIDS are often and mistakenly interchanged, AIDS is the final and fatal stage of HIV in which the immune system becomes so weak that infections that individuals with healthy defenses can fight off take hold.

Dr. Beatrice Hahn is credited with discovering the origins of HIV from the Simian immunodeficiency virus (known as SIVcpz). Hahn used the decades of observational data from Gombe combined with new molecular genetic technology to discover the link. The SIVcpz virus, which may not be fatal to chimps and other primates, had mutated, or changed, to become HIV, which is deadly to humans. Hahn's current research focuses on developing a human-based AIDS vaccine. More recently, a different virus, similar to AIDS, has been discovered among deceased chimps at Gombe. While scientists are not yet sure what is happening at the molecular level, it is preliminarily believed that encroaching human populations surrounding the Reserve may play

Dian Fossey's observations of Rwandan mountain gorillas lasted for eighteen years; she was also a vocal opponent of poaching and tourism in the area, calling for the preservation of gorilla habitats.

a part in the inter-species transfer. Gombe offers excellent wild lab conditions, including data on multiple generations, subjects accustomed to researchers, and developed relationships with Tanzanians.

Advances in genetic technology also provide the opportunity to answer questions that have long been asked at Gombe. For instance, Goodall and other researchers knew that determining Gombe chimp paternity would be important to understanding social structure, dominance, and hierarchies. How did the position of alpha, or top male, in a chimpanzee group correlate, or connect, to average number of offspring parented?

While working on her PhD at the University of Minnesota in Ecology, Evolution, and Behavior, Emily Wroblewski studied relationships at Gombe. Using fecal samples, the young scientist was able to build the paternal family tree and trace relations between the male adult and infant chimps. Wroblewski's work indicated that higher-ranking males do in fact father many offspring; however, lower-ranking chimps also fare well. Often, they will form partnerships with lower-ranking females and this, in turn, helps them to successfully reproduce at higher rates. Although Goodall made a preliminary observation of the same ilk more than two decades prior, Wroblewski's DNA evidence confirmed her speculation.

About thirty years ago, the Research Center began studying baboon populations in addition to the Kasekala chimps. Anthony Collins, a Scottish scientist, oversees that project along with directing some of the Center's ecotourism efforts.

BOOKS AND MEMOIRS

Goodall's career has resulted not only in multiple organizations, research projects, and conservationist efforts, but in many publications and books. She began in the August 1963 edition of *National Geographic* magazine with the article "My Life Among Wild Chimpanzees" in which she detailed her first few years in Gombe studying David Greybeard and the other chimps. In 1971, she coauthored the book *Innocent Killers* with her first husband, the nature photographer Hugo van Lanwick. Her next publication, the book *In the Shadow of Man*, chronicled her early years of fieldwork in Gombe. Published in over forty-eight languages, Goodall took her readers first through her arrival to Africa and then to her first visit to Gombe. She went on to detail the chimpanzees' precise and individual characteristics along with her major findings and observations.

Subsequent books, including *In the Shadow of Man* and *Through a Window: My Thirty Years with the Chimpanzees of Gombe*, have allowed Goodall to expand on her arguments, experiences, and scientific theories. In *In the Shadow of Man*, published in 1971, Goodall detailed her first ten years in Gombe, from 1960 until 1970. *Through a Window* (1990) created a more vivid and in-depth analysis, building on Goodall's then thirty years of experience in Gombe.

Also, Goodall has written multiple books for children and appeared in many films and documentaries including the Oscar-nominated HBO film, *Chimps, So Like Us* in 1990. Goodall also voiced her character on the animated series *The Wild Thornberrys*.

Spirituality

As she got older, Goodall continued to focus on science and theory, but she also published more autobiographical, reflective works. In 1999, she released *Reason for Hope: A Spiritual Journey*, which details her strong belief that hope lies in human action. The human brain, Goodall argues, contains an immense capacity for both aggression and love. Humans' ability to invent and innovate allows for productive interaction with nature. Her second reason for hope is the resiliency of nature. She

CHARLOTTE UHLENBROEK

Born in England, young Charlotte Uhlenbroek spent ten days in her birth country before moving with her parents to Ghana. At the age of five, her family moved to Kathmandu, Nepal, where a love for animals blossomed. She spent her childhood attempting to help Nepalese stray dogs. As a teenager, Uhlenbroek traveled to Tanzania where she visited the Gombe Stream Research Center. Later she recalled, "I remember thinking immediately that I'd love to work in a place like this. Little did I know that a few years later I would be doing exactly that." Uhlenbroek studied Zoology and Psychology at Bristol University and then went on to facilitate a chimpanzee conservation project sponsored by Jane Goodall in Burundi. She later studied chimp communication at Gombe. Uhlenbroek has appeared on numerous programs through the British Broadcasting Chanel (BBC) including *Dawn to Dusk* and *Chimpanzee Diaries*. David Attenborough, renowned British naturalist and television personality, has even identified Uhlenbroek as his successor in an interview, noting his belief in her skills and aptitudes.

Uhlenbroek has also written several books and is an activist against primate experimentation. She advocates for public involvement in conservation efforts, noting in an interview,

I am a great believer in the power of ordinary people to effect change ... people need to aid wildlife protection in other ways too, such as by supporting charities or buying fairly traded goods that encourage the sustainable use of natural resources. Educating ourselves about what the pressures are on wildlife and the environment makes us much more effective at campaigning and supporting conservation projects.

reminds her readers that nature can recover from almost any human invasion, the miracle of species returning from the brink of extinction and habitats recovering from years of pollution and toxins. Goodall is vocally spiritual and has written and discussed how her faith and science go hand in hand. Because of her beliefs, she points out, she has found a place in the universe, a way to peacefully endure tragedies and chaos, and ways to conceptualize hopeful futures and the positive potential that humans can have with the ecological world. Her most recent works have branched out to other aspects of biological, conservation, and zoology. *Harvest for Hope,* published in 2005, examines where our food comes from and what people can do to ensure that their food does not originate through the exploitation of people. *Hope for Animals and Their World* (2009) examines endangered species, habitat destruction, and steps for regeneration. Her most recent publication, *Seeds of Hope,* explores biology and lessons from the world of plants. When asked in an interview with *Smithsonian* magazine, Goodall was asked what prompted her to explore the world of plants. She recalled,

“ *The tree I had in the garden as a child, my beech tree, I used to climb up there and spend hours. I took my homework up there, my books, I went up there if I was sad, and it just felt very good to be up there among the green leaves and the birds and the sky. All around our home in Bournemouth, [England], there were wild cliffs with trees, and pines, and I just came to really love trees. Of course, reading books about Tarzan, I fell in love with the jungle—as we called it then—and that was part of my dream of wanting to go to Africa, to be out in the forest.* **”**

A LASTING LEGACY

Often when Goodall gives lectures and interviews, she likes to tell the story of Old Man the chimpanzee. Named for his ragged appearance and not his actual age, Old Man spent much of his youth in a biomedical research lab where he was mistreated and abused. At the age of twelve, he was placed in a zoo with other chimpanzees. The chimp zookeeper was warned that because of his dark past, Old Man did not like humans and could be violent towards them. However, slowly, the caretaker built a trusting relationship with the scarred chimp; he brought bananas and groomed Old Man. One day, while cleaning the enclosure, the zookeeper fell and scared an infant chimpanzee. The mother, sensing danger for her baby, rushed over and bit his neck; two other chimps also began biting and attacking him. When Old Man charged over, his hair bristled in a classic aggressive chimpanzee manner, the caretaker feared that it would be the end, that the angry, mistreated chimp would kill him. However, Old Man pushed the other chimps away so that the zookeeper was able to crawl away. When Goodall tells this story, she finishes with, "If a chimpanzee can reach across the species gap to save a man, surely we can reach out to help the chimpanzee."

Goodall continues to advocate for the mistreated, for the ignored, and for the broken. In *Reason For Hope,* she muses on what the future holds both for her and the globe,

❝ *Of course, as long as I live I shall continue to spread awareness about the true nature of animals, the extent of their suffering, and our responsibilities toward them. I shall go on speaking out against animal experimentation, intensive farming, fur farming, trapping, sport hunting,* *the exploitation of animals in entertainment, as beasts of burden, and as pets ... What does lie ahead? It cannot be denied that our human societies are cursed with war and crime and violence; it has been thus from the start of recorded history. It seems that every time some troubled part of the world solves its ideological, ethnic, or territorial problems, fighting flares up somewhere else ... So what can we do? When I address groups of youth, I tell them that there is a lot we can do, each and every one of us, just by trying to make the world around us a better place. It can be very simple: we can make a sad or lonely person smile; we can make a miserable dog wag his tail or a cat purr; we can give water to a little wilting plant. We cannot solve all the problems of the world, but we can often do something about the problems under our noses. We can't save all the starving children and beggars of Africa, of Asia, but what about the street children, the homeless, the aged in our own hometown?* ❞

Today, Goodall's theories are accepted worldwide. From a young girl with dreams of Africa to a young woman whose appearance was discussed more than her contributions, Goodall became a global champion for conservation and animal rights. She still misses the early years at Gombe, but acknowledges that things have changed. When asked in an interview if she missed the chimps, Goodall replied,

❝ *I do. A lot of it is just being out in the forest. But Gombe is very different for me, now. There are more tourists, wider trails, so it's hard to be with chimps on your own.*

We don't manage the tourism, so although there are rules about how many tourists can be with the chimps, the rules get interpreted in such a way that you can have three groups of six tourists all clustered around one chimp and her offspring. It's very disturbing to me. But the chimps don't seem to care that much. **"**

Now in her eighties, Goodall believes that one of her lasting legacies is a simple one: "Helping people to understand who animals really are." She advises that everyone should "connect the heart and brain, get into nature. When you have a relationship with some kind of animal it's very grounding."

CHRONOLOGY

1934 Valerie Jane Goodall is born on April 3 in London, England.

1942 Mortimer and Vanne Morris-Goodall, Jane's parents, divorce.

1945 World War II ends.

1957 Goodall takes her first trip to Africa to visit a friend's family farm in Kenya.

1960 Goodall begins studying chimpanzees at Gombe Stream Reserve at the request of Louis Leakey; observes David Greybeard using tools to collect termites and other chimps eating meat.

1961 The National Geographic Society awards Goodall with her first grant.

1962 Goodall begins her PhD at Cambridge.

1963 Goodall's first article, "My Life among the Chimpanzees," appears in *National Geographic* magazine.

1964 Goodall and wildlife photographer Hugo Van Lawick are married on March 28.

1965 Gombe Stream Research Center is founded; Goodall graduates with a PhD in Ethology from Cambridge University.

1967	Goodall gives birth to son Hugo Eric Louis van Lawick, nicknamed "Grub."
1971	Jane publishes her first book, *In the Shadow of Man*.
1974	The Four Year War begins between the Kasakela and Kahema groups; van Lawick and Goodall divorce amicably.
1975	Four students are kidnapped by Zairian rebels and outside researchers are not allowed in Gombe until 1989; Goodall marries her second husband, Derek Bryceson.
1977	The Jane Goodall Institute is founded.
1980	Jane's husband dies.
1990	Jane publishes *Through a Window*.
1991	Jane founds youth action program Roots & Shoots.
1994	TACARE is founded.
1999	Reason for *Hope: A Spiritual Journey* is published.
2001	Vanne Goodall dies.
2002	Goodall is named a United Nations Messenger of Peace.
2003	Goodall is invested as Dame of the British Empire by Prince Charles.
2006	The Jane Goodall Institute celebrates its 30th anniversary.

GLOSSARY

allies The nations that fought together against Germany in World War I or World War II.

altruism Feelings and behavior that show a desire to help other people.

animal husbandry A kind of farming in which people raise animals for meat, milk, eggs, etc.

arboreal Living in or often found in trees.

Axis countries The nations that allied with Germany in World War I or World War II.

conscription Forcing people by law to serve in the armed forces.

convection Movement in a gas or liquid in which the warmer parts move up and the colder parts move down.

embassy A group of people who work under an ambassador and represent their country in a foreign country.

genocide The deliberate killing of people who belong to a particular racial, political, or cultural group.

genus A group of related animals or plants that includes several or many different species.

hominid Any of a family of two-footed primate mammals that includes recent humans together with extinct ancestral and related forms.

Homo sapiens The species of human beings that exist today.

in utero In the uterus.

lithosphere The solid part of a celestial body (as the earth).

malaria A serious disease that causes chills and fever and that is passed from one person to another by the bite of mosquitoes.

matriarchy A family, group, or government controlled by a woman or a group of women.

menagerie A collection of animals kept especially to be shown to the public.

natural selection The process by which plants and animals that can adapt to changes in their environment are able to survive and reproduce while those that cannot adapt do not survive.

Oman Country on the Arabian Peninsula bordering on Arabian Sea.

paleoanthropology A branch of anthropology dealing with fossil hominids.

parliament An elected group of people who are responsible for making laws.

prime minister The head of the government in some countries.

radioactivity The property possessed by some elements of emitting energetic particles.

rift A deep crack or opening in the ground or a rock.

socialism A way of organizing a society in which industries are owned by the government rather than by individual people and companies.

spectrometer An instrument used for measuring wavelengths of light spectra.

subsistence farmers Farming that provides all the goods required by the farmer and farmer's family to use, without an extra to sell.

Swahili A language widely used in East Africa and the Congo region.

thesis A long, written work of research that is done to earn a degree at a university.

Treaty of Versailles Peace treaty at the end of World War I.

vaccine An injection that is used to protect against a particular disease.

vertebrate Having a spinal column.

zoology The branch of science that involves the study of animals and animal behavior.

FURTHER INFORMATION

BOOKS

Goodall, Jane. *My Life with the Chimpanzees*. New York: Simon and Schuster, 1996.

Goodall, Jane and Phillip Berman. *Reason for Hope: A Spiritual Journey*. New York: Grand Central Publishing, 2000.

Ottaviani, Jim. *Primates: The Fearless Science of Jane Goodall, Dian Fossey, and Biruté Galdikas*. New York: First Second, 2013.

WEBSITES

Interactive Human Evolution Timeline

http://humanorigins.si.edu/evidence/human-evolution-timeline-interactive

Explore the climate and geographical conditions in the evolution of different hominid species and human ancestors.

Jane Goodall Timeline

http://www.janegoodall.ca/goodall-bio-timeline.php

An interactive timeline that details Jane Goodall's life and research.

Roots & Shoots

https://www.rootsandshoots.org/about

Jane Goodall's youth-based conservation and action program.

VIDEOS

How humans and animals can live together

https://www.ted.com/talks/jane_goodall_at_tedglobal_07

In this TED talk video, Jane Goodall discusses her community projects that enable villagers and primates to live near one another peacefully.

What separates us from chimpanzees?

https://www.ted.com/talks/jane_goodall_on_
what_separates_us_from_the_apes

In this TED talk video, Jane Goodall discusses the similarities between chimps and humans, and how people can use those differences for good.

BIBLIOGRAPHY

"About HIV/AIDS." Centers for Disease Control and Prevention. 2016. July 7, 2016. http://www.cdc.gov/hiv/basics/whatishiv.html.

Bardhan-Quallen, Sudipta. *Up Close: Jane Goodall*. England: Penguin Books, 2008. BBC History. "Fact File: Women's Land Army." October 15, 2014. http://www.bbc.co.uk/history/ww2peopleswar/timeline/factfiles/nonflash/a6652055.shtml.

BBC History. "Fact File: Women's Auxillary Air Force." October 15, 2014. http://www.bbc.co.uk/history/ww2peopleswar/timeline/factfiles/nonflash/a6649932.shtml?sectionId=0&articleId=6649932.

Black, Amy, and Stephen Brooke. "The Labour Party, Women, and the Problem of Gender, 1951–1966." *The Journal of British Studies J. Br. Stud.* 36, no. 04 (October 1997): 419-52. doi:10.1086/386144.

"Called 'Trimates,' Three Bold Women Shaped Their Field." *Science*. April 16, 1993. http://science.sciencemag.org/content/260/5106/420.pdf-extract.

Castelow, Ellen. "The 1950s Housewife." Retrieved April 29, 2016. http://www.historic uk.com/CultureUK/The-1950s-Housewife.

Embassy of the Republic of Kenya in Japan. "A Brief History on Kenya." Accessed April 30, 2016. http://www.kenyarep-jp.com/kenya/history_e.html.

"Emily Wroblewski." The Parham Lab. Accessed June 08, 2016. http://
web.stanford.edu/group/parhamlab/members/emily-wroblewski.

Gardiner, Juliet. "The Story of Women in the 1950s." September 9, 2015.
http://www.historytoday.com/reviews/story-women-1950s

Goodall, Jane. *Jane Goodall: 50 Years at Gombe*. New York: Stewart,
Tabori & Chang, 2010.

"Guide to the Honours." BBC News June 10, 2015. http://www.bbc.com/
news/uk-11990088.

Guilder, George. "Women in the Work Force." Septermber 1986. http://
www.theatlantic.com/magazine/archive/1986/09/women-in-the-
work-force/304924.

Harris, Carol. "Women Under Fire in World War Two." February
17, 2011. http://www.bbc.co.uk/history/british/britain_wwtwo/
women_at_war_01.shtml.

History.com Staff. "Britain and France declare war on Germany."
Retrieved on April 19, 2016. http://www.history.com/this-day-in-
history/britain-and-france-declare-war-on-germany.

History.com Staff. "The Holocaust." Retrieved April 30, 2016. http://
www.history.com/topics/world-war-ii/the-holocaust.

Institute of Geosciences and Earth Resources. "The Ethiopian Rift
Valley." Retrieved May 6, 2016. http://ethiopianrift.igg.cnr.it/rift%20
valley%20significance.htm.

May, Elaine Tyler. "Women and Work." Interview. *Tupperware*.
Transcript. PBS. http://www.pbs.org/wgbh/americanexperience/
features/interview/tupperware-may.

Onion, Rebecca. "Unclaimed Treasures of Science." *Slate.* July 13, 2014. http://www.slate.com/articles/health_and_science/science/2014/07/ women_in_science_technology_engineering_math_history_of_ advocacy_from_1940.html.

Our Africa. "Great Rift." Retrieved May 6, 2016. http://www.our-africa. org/tanzania/great-rift.

Quammen, David. "Fifty Years at Gombe." *National Geographic.* October 2010. http://ngm.nationalgeographic.com/print/2010/10/ jane-goodall/quammen-text.

Reader, John. *Missing Links: In Search of Human Origins.* Oxford: Oxford University Press, 2011.

Sarmiento, Esteban E., G. J. Sawyer, Richard Milner, and Viktor Deak. *The Last Human: A Guide to Twenty-two Species of Extinct Humans.* New Haven: Yale University Press, 2007.

Tanzania National Parks. "Gombe Stream National Park." Accessed June 08, 2016. http://www.tanzaniaparks.com/gombe.html.

Trueman, C.N. "The Women's Land Army." April 20, 2015. http:// www.historylearningsite.co.uk/world-war-two/world-war-two-in-western- europe/britains-home-front-in-world-war-two/the-womens-land-army.

Uhlenbroek, Charlotte. Charlotte Uhlenbroek, Natural World Hero. Accessed June 08, 2016. https://www.naturalworldsafaris.com/ natural-world-heroes/charlotte-uhlenbroek.

"US Inflation Calculator." US Inflation Calculator. Accessed June 08, 2016. http://www.usinflationcalculator.com.

INDEX

Page numbers in **boldface** are illustrations. Entries in **boldface** are glossary terms.

ABOUT THE AUTHOR

Megan Mitchell is a former biology educator and current graduate student at the University of California, Davis. There, she studies how gardens in schools affect teachers and students. For her bachelor's degree, Mitchell attended the University of Texas where she worked as a research assistant in The Children's Research Lab. She has written many lesson plans for her classroom and designed middle school science curriculum. *Jane Goodall: Primatologist and UN Messenger of Peace* is her second full-length book. Mitchell loves gardening, hiking, reading, and performing scientific experiments. She hopes that one day genetics will be able to explain why her two dogs, Butters and Toast, have such silly personalities.